GREAT
SPORTING
WISDOM

JOHN SCALLY
GREAT SPORTING WISDOM

CollinsWillow

An Imprint of HarperCollinsPublishers

To Sheila, Aine, James,
Liam and Fiona Finneran

Acknowledgements

Thanks to all the sports personalities quoted who never fail to entertain with their verbal skills.

Thanks also to Richard Jolley for his excellent cartoons.

Finally, my gratitude to the publishers CollinsWillow, especially Michael Doggart and Tom Whiting for their interest and encouragement.

Published in 1996
by CollinsWillow
an imprint of HarperCollins*Publishers*
London

© John Scally 1996

1 3 5 7 9 8 6 4 2

A CIP catalogue record for this book is available from the British Library

ISBN 0 00 218733 7

Printed in Great Britain by
Caledonian International Book Manufacturing Ltd

Contents

Introduction

The Good, The Glad and The Wordy

Chapter One: Athletic Aberrations 12

Chapter Two: Baseball Bloomers 20

Chapter Three: Basketball Babel.................................... 33

Chapter Four: Board and Card Games 36

Chapter Five: Boxing Barbs 40

Chapter Six: Pedal to the Metal 48

Chapter Seven: Cricket Classics 55

Chapter Eight: Football's Fun and Frolics 72

Chapter Nine: Golfing Gems 96

Chapter Ten: Horse Racing Hoots 118

Chapter Eleven: Ruck and Roll 137

Chapter Twelve: Snooker from the Lip 149

Chapter Thirteen: Tennis Theatricals 159

Chapter Fourteen: Sporting Miscellany...................... 166

Great Sporting Supermouths of our Time

Chapter Fifteen: Walker the Talker 180

Chapter Sixteen: The Lowe-Down 183

Chapter Seventeen: On the Great Vine 187

Chapter Eighteen: The Golden Foot in Mouth Award.....189

Introduction

In 1906 Ambrose Bierce defined quotation as 'the act of repeating erroneously the words of another. The words erroneously repeated.' Down through history much has been said and written about the people and events that have shaped the sporting world. This book assembles some of the most commonly misquoted and misattributed of those sporting quotations.

Humour is a difficult thing to define. What reduces one person to helpless laughter may leave another indifferent. And what makes a funny quote? The context can be crucial.

In normal circumstances the following would not be of great interest: 'Sharp are currently working on bringing 3D TV into your living-rooms. Mr Koshima hopes it will be so realistic that viewers will have to duck when Eric Cantona takes a shot.'

However, what makes this press release from Manchester United's sponsors such a gem is that it was issued just before Cantona's flying kick at a Crystal Palace fan. Of course, Cantona has carved a special niche for himself in this field with the immortal 'When the seagulls follow the trawler, it is because they think sardines will be thrown into the sea.' No doubt this remark will be the subject of PhD theses in years to come in such disparate disciplines as philosophy, Anglo-French literature and sporting psychology.

The quote 'Because we are dressed in black and white, the red, yellow, green, brown, blue and pink of the balls appeal to us' may not seem very noteworthy. It becomes interesting when the source is revealed as Mother John Baptist of the Benedictine Order of the Adorers of the Sacred Heart of Jesus of Montmartre, who pray for the one hundred martyrs of the Reformation, during a snooker competition among the sisters to raise funds for their London convent.

Innuendo is another favoured verbal weapon in sporting quotes. An example is a remark, often attributed to Jilly Cooper, about a different form of sailing game: 'I never liked sailing men. They yell blue murder at you all day, but then, when the boat is moored, the whisky comes out, "Captain Bligh" turns into Casanova and is all ready to play *deck coitus*.'

In 1890 Samuel Butler observed: 'It is bad enough to see one's own good things fathered on other people, but it is worse to have other people's rubbish fathered upon oneself.' Received wisdom is often incorrect. Cary Grant boasted: 'I improve on misquotation.' This book may also serve as an arbitration facility for long-standing disputes about who said what. The target audience is any reader with a sense of humour, or an eye for the eccentric or simply ridiculous, but obviously this will mean more to the sports enthusiast. One preliminary warning – the truth is often funnier than fiction.

John Scally
Rathmines, Dublin

PART ONE

THE GOOD, THE GLAD AND THE WORDY

1

Athletic Aberrations

Robert Burns once stated: 'I like to have quotations ready for every occasion . . . they save one the trouble of finding expression adequate to one's feelings.' At its best, athletics has the power to make the pulse miss a beat. Whatever your sporting fancy, this collection of quotations re-creates the unique excitement, drama and unpredictability of athletics in the words of the sport's practitioners. Anyone who's anyone in the athletics game may find themselves quoted here in their scurrilous, unguarded, rude and humorous moments. A newspaper is rather caustically defined by George Bernard Shaw as a device 'unable to distinguish between a bicycle accident and the collapse of civilisation.' Hence it is no surprise that the media presence in this section is very strong.

1. On the track

Misplaced Confidence
The difference between me and other athletes who go to the Olympics is that I go to win and they go to compete.
David Bedford, long-distance runner, before the Munich Olympics. He only came sixth!

Heavy Breather
The only reason I would take up jogging is so that I could hear heavy breathing again.
Erma Bombeck

Fall Of The Titans
The most famous collision since the Titanic and the iceberg.
Pat Butcher on Zola Budd's tripping of Mary Decker in the 1984 Olympics

Amongst Women
My secrets? I don't know – maybe ladies?
Mexican marathon man Dionicio Ceron on the key to his success

Health-Conscious
Go jogging? What, and get hit by a meteor?
Robert Benchley

CAUTION!
METEORITES

The Power Of Love
I never jog. Love is still a better and more pleasurable sport.
   Cary Grant

Race
We should be thankful to lynch mobs. I've got a brother who can run a half-mile faster than any white boy in the world.
   Dick Gregory

Handicap
My leotard got twisted and stuck right up my bottom just as I was getting to the hurdle. It was a bit of an unwanted distraction, really.
   Sally Gunnell, unhappy at encountering unexpected problems in her 1993 World Championship semi-final

You Don't Say
Early rounds of an athletics meeting are called heats, because that is when the competition begins to heat up.
   Colin M. Jarman

A Racing Certainty
The race is not always to the swift, but that is where to look.
   Hugh E. Keough

Close Shave
Italian men and Russian women don't shave before a race.
   Eddy Ottoz

Bias
The decathlon is nine Mickey Mouse events and the 1500 metres.
   Steve Ovett

Incentive
I'm Jewish. I don't work out. If God wanted us to bend over he'd put diamonds on the floor.
   Joan Rivers

Missing The Target
The athletic facilities situation is a mess. Girls still haven't figured out how to use the urinals.
   John Roberts

Elementary, My Dear Watson
In running, you have to be suspicious when you line up against girls with moustaches.
  Maree Holland

Medical Advice
My doctor told me my jogging could add years to my life. I told him 'Yeah, since I began, I already feel ten years older!'
  Lee Trevino

Early Risers
Jogging is for people who aren't intelligent enough to watch Breakfast TV.
  Victoria Wood

Testing Positive
If she [Diane Modahl] was as much over the limit as the test supposes, she would be a big girl with a deep voice and beard. We'd all be calling her Barry White.
  Tony Jarrett

High Power
Nature's attempt [Vladimir Kuts - Olympic 5000 & 10000m champion] at an engine in boots.
  A. P. Herbert

Wired For Speed
I'm studying to be an electronics engineer. I put wires in my legs.
Wilson Kipketer after winning the 800m gold at the 1995 World Championships

Mathematics Made Complicated
I've got ten pairs of training shoes. One for every day of the week.
Samantha Fox, ex-Page Three Girl

Requirements
Women need a firm bra, not one of the flimsy all-elastic ones. That's especially true if you have large breasts. Otherwise they'll bounce and you'll always be waiting for them to come down before you take your step.
Nine Kuscsik

2. Field Of Dreams

Expensive Education
Experience is a good teacher, but she sends in terrific bills.
Minna Antrim

Muscle
People think of me as the Incredible Hulk.
Fatima Whitbread

The Hands That Rock The Cradle
To be an Olympic champion, I am convinced you must choose your parents carefully.
Per-Olaf Astrand, Swedish athletic researcher

Idiotic
Athletic sports, save in the case of young boys, are designed for idiots.
George Nathan

Amateur Ethos
A proper definition of an amateur sportsman today is one who accepts cash, not cheques.
Jack Kelly

High Profile
Our athletes are flying the flagship for British sport.
Fatima Whitbread

Elegance
Watching the Russian female shot-putters is like watching an eighteen-stone ballet dancer.
David Campbell

Hidden Talents
Somewhere inside that flabby body [Geoff Capes'] was an athlete trying to get out.
Stuart Storey

High Flyers
If you want a track team to win the high jump, you find one person who can jump seven feet, not seven people who can each jump one foot.
Frederick E. Terman

Vogue
The only time our girls looked good in Munich was in the discotheque, between 9 and 11 every night.
US Olympic coach

Realism
I know I'm no Kim Basinger – but she can't throw the javelin.
Fatima Whitbread

Birth Control
The [Olympic] Games need to take the Pill before the sporting explosion gets entirely out of hand.
Peter Wilson

3. Soundbytes

Job Opportunities
If you're a sporting star, you're a sporting star. If you don't quite make it, you become a coach. If you can't coach, you become a journalist. If you can't spell, you introduce *Grandstand* on a Saturday afternoon.
Desmond Lynam

Darwin Revisited
Tonight, a special *Horizon* programme, Survival of the Fartest . . . Fastest.
> *Richard Baker from the BBC cassette Sporting Gaffes*

Sequence Of Events
That performance would have won him the Olympic gold medal in the championship four years ago, which he won anyway.
> *Desmond Lynam, talking about Sebastian Coe*

Get To The Bottom Of It
Harvey Glance, the black American sprinter, with the white top and black bottom.
> *Ron Pickering*

A Change Of Plan
When the pace is slow, sometimes the athletes will make a move they hadn't planned to make earlier in the race than they planned to do it.
> *Brendan Foster*

Insight
Watch the time – it gives you a good indication of how fast they are running.
> *Ron Pickering*

Carried Away
Anything that matters so much to David Coleman, you realise, doesn't matter so much at all.
> *Clive James*

Des -ire
Desmond Lynam is so laid back, he's almost horizontal – which is exactly how his legions of fantasising housewifely fans imagine him to be.
> *Frank Keating*

The Invisible Woman
Zola Budd, so small, so waif-like, you literally cannot see her; but there she is.
> *Alan Parry*

Trivia
The world's fastest woman is an expert cook.
  Daily Graphic *headline after Fanny Blankers-Koen won*
  Olympic gold in 1948

Power To All Our Friends
The man [Henry Rono] with asbestos lungs.
  Ron Pickering

2

Baseball Bloomers

Anyone who loses sleep worrying about the meaning of life will not seek answers among baseball practitioners. But to those who love the game, baseball is the meaning of life. For lovers of the absurd, outrageous and totally bizarre, this selection of sporting quotes could make the proverbial cat laugh. A pot pourri of double entendres, satirical quips and unintentional puns from the tongues of a sporting elite. Reading pleasure for the mischievous and warped.

1. The All-American Game

Hype
Calling it the World Series must impress the world as an example of America's modesty.
Anon

Run That By Me Again
No wonder nobody comes here [a crowded New York restaurant] to eat – it's too crowded.
Yogi Berra, New York Yankees

Lords and Masters
Baseball must be a great game to survive the people who run it.
Arthur Daley, sportswriter

Parental Control
I think Little League is all right: it keeps the parents off the street.
Rocky Bridges, Minor League manager

You Don't Say
[Orel] Hershiser is the only Major League player to have two consecutive pronouns in his surname.
Roger Angell, sportswriter

Descent of the Apes
'Babe' Ruth wasn't born – the sonofabitch fell from a tree.
Joe Duggan, New York Yankees

Ruth
The Ruth is mighty and shall prevail.
Heywood Broun

Crowd Puller
Houston has its largest crowd of the night here this evening.
Jerry Coleman, (in)famous commentator

Billy the Kid
A baseball fan has the digestive apparatus of a billy goat. He can – and does – devour any set of diamond statistics with insatiable appetite and then nuzzles hungrily for more.
Arthur Daley

Speed
The Mets [baseball team] has come along slow, but fast!
Casey Stengel

Beauty and the Beast
1. It's no fun being married to an electric light.
   Joe DiMaggio on his marriage to Marilyn Monroe

2. I don't know if it's good for baseball, but it sure beats
the hell out of rooming with Phil Rizzuto!
   Yogi Berra on the marriage

3. Why marry a ball player when you can have the
whole team?
   Mae West on the marriage

4. It proves that no man can be a success in two
national pastimes.
   Oscar Levant on the break-up of the marriage

The Demon Drink
Two of the pall-bearers at Babe Ruth's funeral in August 1948
were teammates – pitcher Waite Hoyt (himself an alcoholic)
and Third Baseman Joe Duggan. As they carried out their
duties, *Duggan whispered:* 'I'd give $100 for a cold beer'. *Hoyt
replied:* 'So would the Babe.'

Back to Basics
When all is said and done, sexual intercourse is the only thing worth a fuck.
Casey Stengel attributed

Night and Day
Los Angeles is a town where you can watch night baseball almost any afternoon.
Anon

Business and Pleasure
A baseball game is twice as much fun if you're seeing it on the company's time.
William Feather, publisher

What A Waste?
After spending four years as a college star, he was a failure at pro baseball. In fact, all he had to show for it was an education.
Anon

Patriotism
I take a national view of the American League and an American view of the National League.
Hubert Humphrey, former US Vice-President

Home Advantage
The good thing about playing for Cleveland that is you don't have to make road trips there.
Jay Johnstone, Cleveland Indians

Shorts
Ballet is the fairies' baseball.
Oscar Levant, humourist

COD
How does he want it? Cash or green stamps?
Billy Martin, New York Yankees, when told he was facing a $1 million lawsuit

Results
There are no prizes for winning the first half.
Steve Rogers, sportswriter

Absolutely Fabulous
We've got an absolutely perfect day here at Desert Sun Stadium, and we're told it's going to be an even more perfect day tomorrow.
Jerry Coleman

Speaking Proper
Old Diz knows the King's English. And not only that. I also know the Queen is English.
Dizzy Dean, (in)famous commentator

The Final Nail In The Coffin
The only real way you know you've been fired, is when you arrive at the ball park and find your name has been scratched from the parking list.
Billy Martin

Narcissism
[Charlie O.] Finley is a self-made man who worships his creator.
Jim Murray, sportswriter

Mixed Blessing
The advantage of playing in New York is in getting to watch Reggie Jackson play every day. And the disadvantage is in getting to watch Reggie Jackson play every day.
Craig Nettles, New York Yankees

Not Like The Military
Close doesn't count in baseball. Close only counts in horseshoes and grenades.
Frank Robinson, Baltimore Orioles

The Man In The Middle
Pity the woman who marries a baseball umpire and has to have a man around the house who is always right.
Anon

To Russia With Love
You must give the Russians credit, they haven't claimed yet that they invented baseball.
Ian Rosenberg, humourist

Distinguished Performer
If you come down to Ebbets Field today, you won't have any
trouble recognising me. My number is 42.
  *Jackie Robinson to his wife, before becoming the first
  Afro-American player in the Major League*

A Thankless Task
It's like being the president of the Flat Earth Society.
  *Don Smallwood, the President of the British Baseball Federation
  on the low interest in the sport in the UK*

Envy
There's two kinds of ball players – prospects and suspects.
And suspects don't like prospects.
  Anon

Women Trouble
There is no reason why the infield should not try to put
the batter off his stride at the critical moment, by neatly-
timed disparagements of his wife's fidelity and his
mother's respectability.
  George Bernard Shaw

2. Players

Persistence
If you don't succeed at first, try second base.
  Anon

Up To Standard
Who said I have no standards? 'Course I have standards!
They may be very low, but at least I have them.
  Yogi Berra

Line Dancing
All right, line up alphabetically according to your height.
  Casey Stengel

Diagnosis
From the way Denny's shaking his head, he's either got an
injured shoulder or a gnat in his eye.
  Jerry Coleman

High Scoring

It took me seventeen years to get three thousand hits. I did it in one afternoon on the golf course.

Henry 'Hank' Aaron, Atlanta Braves

Slow Motion

[Stu] Miller has three speeds – slow, slower and slowest.

Anon

On The Crest Of A Slump

Slumps are like a soft bed – they're easy to get into, and hard to get out of.

Johnny Bench, Cincinnatti Reds

Penetrating Analysis

If the people don't want to come out to the ball park, nobody's gonna stop them.

Yogi Berra

Legs

Who says I treat women badly? Nonsense, I put them on pedestals. It's much easier to look up their skirts that way.

Babe Ruth attributed

Divine Providence
The good Lord was good to me. He gave me a strong body, a strong right arm and a weak mind.
Jay 'Dizzy' Dean, player & sportscaster

Heads Will Roll
There's a fly ball back to centre field. Winfield is going back, back… He hits his head against the wall. It's rolling back towards second base.
Jerry Coleman

Covert Operations
Throwing a fastball by Hank Aaron is like trying to sneak the sunrise past a rooster.
Curt Simmons, Philadelphia Phillies

Highlight Of The Year
Young Frank Pastore may have just pitched the biggest victory of 1979, maybe the biggest victory of the year.
Jerry Coleman

Educating Yogi
You can observe a lot just by watching.
Yogi Berra

Touch Wood
No, I'm not superstitious. I'm afraid it would bring me bad luck.
Babe Ruth

Gratitude
I want to thank everybody who made this night necessary.
Yogi on 'Yogi Berra Night'

Track Record
Rollie Fingers has 35 saves and has a better record than John the Baptist.
Lon Simmons, sportscaster

Plaudits
I couldn't have done half of it [his triumphs] without the players.
Casey Stengel

Percentage Game
Ninety per cent of this game is half-mental.
Jim Wohlford, Milwaukee Brewers

Pretty Woman
A woman to me can be attractive, just by saying yes.
Babe Ruth attributed

Double Trouble
He slides into second with a stand-up double.
Jerry Coleman

Out-standing
A baseball team doesn't run out of time, it runs out of outs.
Robert Gensemer, sportswriter

Sweet Memories
A great catch is just like watching girls go by – the last one
you saw is always the prettiest.
Bob Gibson, St Louis Cardinals

Wage Packet
A homer a day will boost my pay.
Josh Gibson, famous Afro-American league baseball player

Labelling
In a way, an umpire is like a woman. He makes quick
decisions, never reverses them and doesn't think you're safe
when you're out.
Umpire Larry Goetz

Race Relations
Baseball is very big with my people. It figures. It's the only
time we can get to shake a bat at a white man without
starting a riot.
Dick Gregory, comedian

Mixed Blessing
Patience, that's what an older pitcher has that a younger
pitcher doesn't . . . The only trouble is, when you're old, other
people sometimes tend to lose patience with you quicker.
Tommy John, New York Yankees

Room Mate
I don't room with Babe Ruth, I room with his suitcase.
Ping Bodie, New York Yankees

Nothing But The Truth?
I'm not old, I was just born before a lot of other people.
Darrell Evans

Foreign Tongues
Hector Torrez, how can you communicate with Enzo
Herrandez when he speaks Spanish and you speak Mexican?
Jerry Coleman

Victory and Loss
Somebody's gotta win and somebody's gotta lose – and I
believe in letting the other guy lose.
Pete Rose, Cincinnatti Reds and Philadelphia Phillies

Reversal of Fortune
Garry Maddox has turned his life around. He used to be
depressed and miserable. Now he's miserable and depressed.
Harry Kalas, Phillies announcer

Marriage Guidance
When you win you eat better, sleep better and your beer
tastes better. And your wife looks like Gina Lollobrigida.
Johnny Pesky, Boston Red Sox manager

Count Up
That's Hendricks' 19th home run; one more and he hits
double figures.
Jerry Coleman

Tight Fit
Watching Ferando Valenzuela force himself into a Dodger
uniform is like seeing Kate Smith struggling to fit into a pair
of Brooke Shields' designer jeans.
H. G. Reza, sportswriter

Mystery Woman
Who is this 'Babe' Ruth? And what does she do?
George Bernard Shaw

Sound Not Vision
Blind people come to the park just to hear Tom Seaver pitch.
   Reggie Jackson, New York Yankees

Grandma
Only if she was crowding the plate.
   Early Wynn, Cleveland Indians, when asked if he'd throw 'at'
his grandmother

Mixed Messages
We're all sad to see Glen Beckert leave. Before he goes,
though, I hope he stops by so we can kiss him goodbye.
He's that kind of guy.
   Jerry Coleman

3. Media Moments

Time Zone
The way he's swinging the bat, he won't get a hit until the
20th Century.
   Jerry Coleman, referring to Dave Roberts

Medical News
X-rays of Dean's head show nothing.
   Newspaper headline

Time Zone
It's a beautiful day for a night game.
   Frankie Frisch, St Louis Cardinals

Identity Crisis
I don't think so. What paper does he write for?
   Yogi Berra, when asked if he knew Ernest Hemingway, the writer

Against All Odds
Whenever I can, I always watch the Detroit Tigers on the radio.
   Gerald Ford

Educational Problems
At the end of six innings' play, it's Montreal 5, the Expos 3.
   Jerry Coleman

Numerical Disadvantage
There's someone warming up in the bull-pen, but he's obscured by his number.
Jerry Coleman

Iceberg
He [Charlie O. Finley] is so cold-blooded, he ought to make anti-freeze adverts.
Reggie Jackson

It Doesn't Add Up
The Pirates won eight of their 102 losses against the Mets last year.
Ralph Kiner, Pittsburgh Pirates

Papal Bull
Well, that kind of puts the damper on even a Yankee win!
Phil Rizutto – Yankee announcer after announcing the death of Pope Paul VI

Misunderstanding
I remember a reporter asking for a quote, and I didn't know what a quote was. I thought it was some kind of drink.
Joe DiMaggio

Like Father...
Where do folks get off criticising my grammar? I only went up to the second grade, and if I'd gone up to the third, I'd have passed my Old Man.
Dizzy Dean

Dizzy Diet
Sure, I eat what I advertise. Sure, I eat Wheaties for breakfast. A good bowl of Wheaties with bourbon can't be beat.
Dizzy Dean

Dizzyspeak
During a TV commentary: He slud into second.
After his grammar was faulted: What should I have said – sludded?
Dizzy Dean

Muckspreader

You could plant two thousand rows of corn with the fertiliser [Tommy] LaSorda spreads around.

Joe Garagiola, TV commentator

Beyond The Grave

If Casey Stengel were alive today, he'd be spinning in his grave.

Ralph Kiner

3
Basketball Babel

Welcome to Magic's world. The following compilation provides a graphic and entertaining tour of the mind of some of the sport's greatest artists – even the famed 'dream team'. It is a guide or travelogue around the weird ways in which people pursue sporting pleasure. Packed in equal measure with invaluable information are useless trivia and rude comments, containing wry observations about everything and anything.

Prize and Prejudice
The trouble with referees is that they just don't care which side wins.
Tom Canterbury, NBA player

High Flyer
If I were given a change of life, I'd like to see how it would be to live as a mere six-footer.
Wilt 'The Stilt' Chamberlain, Golden State Warriors/LA Lakers

Happy Birthdays
I'm six foot eleven. My birthday covers three days.
Darryl Dawkins, Philadelphia 76ers

Regrets
Sometimes you wake up in the morning and wish your parents had never met.
Bill Fitch, unsuccessful coach, during a losing run

An Honest Crook
I thought I was an honest guy, and just doing what everyone else was doing – bending the rules.
Manny Goldstein, University of New Mexico recruiter

Survival of the Fittest
Quick guys get tired; big guys don't shrink.
Coach Marv Harshman on recruiting players from college

Family Ties
I didn't hire Scott as assistant coach because he's my son. I hired him because I'm married to his mother.
Frank Layden

Keeping Both Options Open
The free throw shot is both easy – and difficult.
Peter Mintoft

Mistaken Identity
I guess I know very little about music. I've just discovered Yoko Ono is a singer. I thought it was Japanese for 'one egg please'.
Anon basketball player

Player Power

We have total discipline in the Lakers' locker room. It's 'yes sir' and 'no sir'. 'Yes sir, Kareem'. 'No sir, Magic'.

Pat Riley, Lakers' coach

Equality of the Sexes

Of course there should be women basketball referees. Incompetence should not be confined to one sex.

Bill Russell, sportswriter

Good Company

It's better to eat caviar with two players than hot dogs with five.

Marcel Souza, sportswriter

Black Magic

He [Magic Johnson] should change his name from Magic to Mystifying.

Mychal Thompson, LA Lakers

Zoo

Basketball, a game which won't be fit for people until they set the basket umbilicus-high and return the giraffes to the zoo.

Ogden Nash, poet and humourist

4
Board and Card Games

C ard and board games have generated a highly enjoyable and varied selection of interesting, informative, intriguing, infuriating and occasionally just witty remarks. For some reason they attract exponents of renowned surrealism, comic genius and savage wit, offering a quirky insight into the sporting psyche as well as some riotous good laughs. The vintage comments range from the classical to the colloquial, from ancient philosophers to today's stars of stage and screen.

Is There A Doctor In The House?
Never play cards with a man named Doc.
  Nelson Algren

Outdoor Pursuits
I'm afraid I play no outdoor games at all, except dominoes.
I have sometimes played dominoes outside a French cafe.
  Oscar Wilde

Small Is Not Beautiful
I failed to make the chess team, because of my height.
  Woody Allen

Blood Is Thicker Than Water
She leads away from aces and neglects to keep my jump bids
alive. But she is still my mother.
  Heywood Brown

Suspicious Minds
Trust everybody – but cut the cards.
  Finley Peter Dunne

Unfair Advantage
A Smith and Wesson beats four aces.
  Michael Enright

Exhaustion
Bridge I regard as only one degree better than absolutely
vacuous conversation, which is certainly the most fatiguing
thing in the world.
  Arthur C. Benson

Waste
As elaborate a waste of human intelligence [chess] as you can
find outside an advertising agency.
  Raymond Chandler

Time Management
Chess is a foolish expedient for making idle people think
they are doing something clever, when they are only
wasting their time.
  George Bernard Shaw

Nothing Compares 2U
Trying to stop [Bobby] Fischer in full flight is like trying to stop a runaway train with a butterfly net.
Liam Fowler

Love Affair
Chess is better than romance.
Bobby Fischer

Exit
When a man's house is on fire, it's time to break off chess.
Thomas Fuller

Equality Of The Sexes
Mixed chess is the ultimate mating game.
Colin M. Jarman

The Feel Bad Factor
I say, let's banish bridge. Let's find some pleasant way of being miserable together.
Don Herold, US humourist

Arrested Development
The only athletic sport I mastered was backgammon.
Douglas Jerrold, playwright

Mistaken Identity
I always thought backgammon was a side of bacon.
Spike Milligan

Revenge Is Sweet
A computer once beat me at chess, but it was no match for me at kick boxing.
Emo Philips

Maverick
She [Joan Collins] has the assurance of someone dealing herself a fifth ace in a card game with children.
Louis T. Stanley

V for Victory
Victory goes to the player who makes the next-to-last mistake.
Savelly Tarkatower

Fair Play
One should always play fairly when one has the winning cards.
Oscar Wilde

Impossible Odds
Fate was kind to him, dealing him a hand of five aces.
Harry Wilson

5

Boxing Barbs

This collection reveals the unquenchable, insatiable wit that smoulders unseen under the mute, impassive faces of the world's toughest men. The result is a wry, idiosyncratic and sometimes bizarre catalogue of comic creations. Perhaps the intensity and sheer brute force of the sport requires a natural human fallout, a spontaneous emission that enables pugilists to get through the physical battle. Comedy serves as a safety valve.

1. The Good

Self-confidence
When you're as great as I am, it's hard to be humble.
Muhammad Ali

Down And Out
Politics is like boxing – you try to knock out your opponents.
Idi Amin

Preliminaries
Marriage is like a boxing card. The preliminaries are
frequently better than the main event.
Anon

Goldfist
My aim is to become another Diego Maradona – the man
with the golden fist.
Frank Bruno

Three In One
If you ever get belted and see three fighters through a haze,
go after the one in the middle. That's what ruined me –
I went after the two guys on the other end.
Max Baer

Family Tree
Charlie Magri has to do well against the unknown Mexican
who comes from a famous family of five boxing brothers.
Harry Carpenter

Discretion
Only the nose knows,
Where the noes goes,
When the door close.
Muhammad Ali, when asked about sex before a fight

Thrilling
It'll be a thrilla, a chilla and a killa when I get the gorilla
in Manila.
*Muhammad Ali's confident prediction before his third clash
with Joe Frazier in 1975*

Behind Every Great Man . . .
I don't know what impressive is, but Joe was impressive tonight.
Marlene Bugner

Crowd Pleaser
When I got into the boxing ring, women used to scream with delight because usually I'd left my shorts in the locker.
Roy Brown

Metaphorically Speaking
That's cricket. You get these sorts of things in boxing.
Frank Bruno, after Jorge Vaca took Lloyd Honeyghan's world title following an accidental clash of heads

Of Biblical Proportions
Joe Bugner: Get me Jesus Christ, I'll fight him tomorrow!
Hugh McIlvanney: Joe, you're only saying that because you know he's got bad hands.

Know What I Mean, Harry?
They said it would last two rounds – they were half wrong, it lasted four.
Harry Carpenter

No Contest
I'm the best heavyweight fighter in Canada and I'll still be the best when I'm dead seven years.
George Chuvalo

Daddy's Girl
This baby was planned. Before conception I had wanted a girl. It's uncanny how I always get what I want.
Chris Eubank

Finnegan's Awake
I know it's said I can't punch, but you should see me putting the cat out at night.
Chris Finnegan

Fair Fight
Sure, the fight was fixed. I fixed it with a right hand.
George Foreman, on his 1994 victory over Michael Moorer

The Eyes Have It
His potatoes kept getting cut eyes.
Reg Gutteridge, on why Henry Cooper quit his
greengrocer's business

Hair Today. Gone Tomorrow
With four sisters about the house, I could never get my hands
on a comb.
'Marvelous' Marvin Hagler on his shaven head

Poetic Justice
I came from a dirt farm. Now I'm filthy rich.
Larry Holmes

Not To Put A Tooth In It
The hardest thing about boxing is picking up your teeth with
a boxing glove on.
Kin Hubbard

Noblesse Oblige
Boxing is described as a 'noble art' because the winner is
usually the first to draw blood on the canvas.
Colin M. Jarman

Womaniser
I enjoy broad-jumping!
Sonny Liston on his hobbies

Relaxation Therapy
I don't like money, actually, but I find it quiets my nerves.
Joe Louis

Affectionate
When women kiss, it always reminds me of prize-fighters shaking hands.
H. L. Mencken

Extra-body Experience
I'd like to borrow Muhammad Ali's body for just forty-eight hours. There are three guys I'd like to beat up and four women I'd like to make love to.
Jim Murray

Rule Of Thumb
Queensbury Rules K.O.
Graffiti

Tunnel Vision
Joe Bugner emerges from the tunnel wearing an outrageous green and white dressing-room.
Gary Richardson

Double Negative
I ain't never liked violence.
Sugar Ray Robinson

Poet's Corner
He has turned defensive boxing into a poetic art. Trouble is, nobody ever knocked anybody out with a poem.
Eddie Shaw, on Herol 'Bomber' Graham

Double Vision
I see two fellows in the ring; I hit the one that isn't there and the one that is there hits me.
Billy Softly

The Arts Show
They called me 'Rembrandt' – because I spent so much time on the canvas.
Bob Hope

Face To Hand
He hit me among my face.
Henny Youngman

Uncertainty
How many chances do I get?
Chuck Wepner, during a standing count in his 1974 clash with Muhammad Ali, when the referee tried to test his senses by asking him what day it was

2. The Bad

Eye To Eye
His gloves, dear. I've never been hit by an eye in my life!
Terry Downes, when asked by a female reporter if he watched his opponent's eyes or gloves

Against The Odds
I've seen George Foreman shadow boxing and the shadow won.
Muhammad Ali

A Vote of No Confidence
A lot of boxing promoters couldn't match the cheeks of
their buttocks.
Mickey Duff – boxing promoter

KO
My toughest fight was with my first wife, and she won every
round.
Muhammad Ali

The Lion And The Lamb
Going into the King's Hall is like going into the lion's den –
you go in like a lion and go out like a lamb.
Barney Eastwood

Slumberland
Terry Downes' face looked as if he had slept on it.
Michael Parkinson

Cut Down To Size
General Gowan of Nigeria: I used to do some boxing.
Muhammad Ali: What did you box? Apples or oranges?

3. The Ugly

Deconstruction
The Great White Hopeless.
*The Boston Globe's verdict on Mike Tyson's comeback
opponent, Peter McNeeley*

Suppression
Joe Bugner was like a volcano that never erupted.
Henry Cooper

In The Eye Of The Beholder
He's [Joe Frazier] so ugly, they ought to donate his face to the
World Wildlife Fund.
Muhammad Ali

Hard Neck
He [John Conteh] has a neck built like a stately home staircase.
Tom Davies

Turning Defence Into Attack
Baroness Summerskill: Mr Cooper, have you looked in the mirror lately and seen the state of your nose?
Henry Cooper: Well, Madam, have you looked in the mirror and seen the state of your nose? Boxing is my excuse. What's yours?

Acid Drops
He's [Sonny Liston] so ugly, that when he cries the tears run down the back of his head.
  Muhammad Ali

6
Pedal to the Metal

The adrenalin of the most exciting and dangerous sport in the world has generated many pithy and quirky quotations which have been a feature of racing parlance for decades. Grand Prix racing represents a curious mixture of stark death and side-splitting humour. The following anthology concentrates exclusively on the brighter side of the sport. The cast includes the magnificent men in the flying speed machines, the fanatics who worship them and cameo appearances from mechanics, drivers' wives and journalists.

1. Danger

The Road To Recovery
I don't know what happened, but I think it was quick. I feel okay. It's a bit difficult to breathe because of my nose and my hand hurts a bit. I'm off to play with the nurses now.
 Rubens Barrichello, following an accident

Casualties
You win some, lose some, wreck some.
 Dale Earnhardt

Sweet Dreams Are Made Of This
The accident didn't hurt me at all. It's an honour to have been under your wheels. I was more worried about you. I have followed you all over, and now I've met you face to face. It really is a dream come true.
 Spectator Ian Neild, who fell under Nigel Mansell's car at the end of the 1992 British Grand Prix

Speed
Brakes only slow you up.
 Tazio Nuvolari

Unwanted Passenger
As well as everything else, there was a lizard in the car. I kept trying to reach it to put it out of the car, but it kept getting away from me. It was still there at the end of practice.
 Ronnie Peterson, on the hazards of practising at Monza

A Nun's Story
I don't know why everything keeps going wrong. Somebody at Team Lotus must have run over a nun.
 Jochen Rindt

Novices
Some of these guys think their mirrors are just for shaving.
 Jody Scheckter, on novices

Clash of the Titans
This is probably what you get when you have one man who believes in God, and another who believes he *is* God.

A member of the McLaren team, on a row between Ayrton Senna and the president of FISA, Jean-Marie Balestre

The Poet Of Speed
Who do you think you are, Nigel Mansell?
No, actually I'm Ayrton Senna.

Conversation between a policeman and Ayrton Senna over speeding

Mixed Metaphors
I wouldn't like to be sitting in Alain Prost's shoes right now.
Barry Sheen

Colour Co-ordination
When the lights go green, he goes red.
Frank Williams on Nigel Mansell

Reasonable Assumption
When a man holds you round the throat, I do not think he has come to apologise.
Ayrton Senna

Forewarned Is Forearmed
I don't mind having an accident when I can see it coming.
  Nigel Mansell

2. Love and Marriage

Big Mistake
Letting my wife go shopping by herself.
  Michael Andretti's reply, when asked the craziest thing he had ever done at Monte Carlo

Happy Families
The secret of a successful marriage is not to be at home too much.
  Colin Chapman

A Man's Friend
Winning is everything. The only ones who remember when you come second are your wife and your dog.
  Damon Hill (Hill also came up with a memorable title for his punk band: Sex Hitler and the Hormones)

Book Of The Month
If all his old girlfriends buy it, it'll be a bestseller.
  'Hot Rod' Hundley's ex-wife, on his autobiography

Love Letters
He would write love letters from all over the world. Well, not actually love letters. They were more technical reports on his car.
  Taormina Rich, ex-girlfriend of James Hunt

Marital Discord
When the car somersaulted at 280 mph when I was going for the record, my only thought was: 'God, the wife is going to kill me for this.'
  Barry Bowles

Sexless Appeal
As for sex, if you look at a driver's harness in the cockpit and realise how the belts squeeze all the blood out of your balls, I wouldn't describe the feeling as at all sexy.
  Keke Rosberg

3. Motoring Miscellany

Damming Indictment
Who Dares Whines.
> The Times' *columnist Simon Barnes' summing up of*
> *Nigel Mansell*

Status Conscious
Executive: I wish the Pope would make you a Cardinal, Enzo.
Enzo Ferrari: Why a Cardinal?
Executive: Because then we'd only have to kiss your ring!

Money, Money, Money
My overdraft is worth a second a lap to me.
> *Innes Ireland*

The Rat
Lauda is worse than Judas. He sells himself for thirty
sausages to our rivals.
> *Enzo Ferrari, after Niki Lauda defected from Ferrari*

Mechanical Problems
Murray Walker: When did you become aware that you had a
puncture, Damon?
Damon Hill: When the tyre went down, Murray.

Capital Start
Racing in Japan was small and so I bought myself a ticket to
Paris, because I thought it was the capital of England.
> *Ukyo Katayama*

Operation Nigel
The brain scan was normal, but I said it was wrong, it has
never been normal.
> *Nigel Mansell, following a crash*

Mum's Not The Word
The fact that I'm the Prime Minister's son doesn't always help.
At Le Mans, for instance, at almost 200 mph down the
Mulsanne Straight, maybe in the rain, Mum can't fix it if
the brakes fail.
> *Mark Thatcher*

Sign Of The Times
You'll notice that most of the mechanics hardly ever touch the engine. They used to be called grease monkeys, but they're keyboard monkeys now.
Nigel Mansell

Divine Intentions
If God wanted us to walk, he'd have given us pogo sticks instead of feet. Feet are made to fit car pedals.
Stirling Moss

The Heart Of The Matter
Louis Stanley: My boy, you have seen my car and my organisation – with my team and my factory, we will make you World Champion.
Clay Regazzoni: Fucka the championship, how mucha you pay?
Exchange between Louis Stanley and Clay Regazzoni

Head On
In one year I travelled 450,000 miles by air. That's eighteen and a half times around the world, or once around Howard Cosell's head.
Jackie Stewart, on US sports broadcaster Howard Cosell

Christlike
Today we celebrate the Resurrection of Christ – and also of Ferrari.
The local priest at Maranello, after Mansell's first win for Ferrari

Initial Shock

On top of that came the CBE, which was most unexpected. I remember picking up this envelope marked '10 Downing Street' and thinking: 'Oh damn, Mark Thatcher's after a drive.'
Robin Herd

Bum Deal

Brilliant in the car, but a pain in the backside out of it.
Frank Williams on Nigel Mansell

7

Cricket Classics

Cricket is the epitome of British reserve and all that goes with the tradition of the 'stiff upper lip'. Hence the phrase 'it's not cricket'. Yet hidden in the undergrowth of the sedate sportsmanlike surface of cricket, which promotes decorum and conformity (with some minor exceptions, such as a well-known captain on *A Question of Sport*) lies a unique discourse. Cricket talk is inevitably fascinating for many reasons, not least of which is that delightful blend of articulate bitchery and polite, well-dressed savagery. The comments represent, in condensed form, the spontaneous venom of some of the thwarted high achievers, charming little darts and wicked little stabs (though sometimes not so little) which are merciless, battering some poor unfortunate without relief or hesitation. The following collection captures the sorrow, pain, elation, despair, affection, hostility and above all, humour, which are the fruits of this consuming passion.

1. Etiquette

The Heart Of The Matter
You can have sex either before cricket or after cricket – the fundamental fact is that cricket must be there at the centre of things.
Harold Pinter

Disaster
I would rather see the whole village dead at my feet than a man bowling in braces.
Adrian Allington

Victory and Defeat
Be magnanimous in defeat and vindictive in victory.
Anon

Just Not Cricket
I don't mind you getting the rabbits [during bowling], but that bugger had myxomatosis.
Anon

Descriptive Powers
A cricket bat is an instrument that looks like a baseball bat run over by a steam-roller.
Anon

Hands-on
It is extremely cold here. The England fielders are keeping their hands in their pockets between balls.
Christopher Martin-Jenkins

Hairy Tale
Dr W. G. Grace
Had hair all over his face.
Lord! How all the people cheered
When a ball got lost in his beard.
E. C. Bentley

The Feet Of A Dancer
Derek Randall stretched like Nureyev for a one-handed catch.
Scyld Berry

Marx and Sparks

He approaches the wicket like Groucho Marx chasing a pretty waitress.

John Arlott, commenting on a peculiar bowling action

Enduring Legacy

He'll regret this to his dying day, if he lives that long.

Sir Neville Cardus

Butchers, Bakers and Century Makers

What are the butchers for?

Actress Pauline Chase, at her first cricket match

A Religious Occasion

The general atmosphere of Lord's is more like that of a prayer meeting than a ball game. It could be that everybody is simply praying for the English team.

Alistair Cooke

Hair Today

When I see a young man who has an expensive and pretty hair-do, I have doubts as to his ability to reach Test standard.

Ted Dexter

Responsible Parenthood

Raman Subba Row: I'm sorry about that, it might have been better if I had kept my legs together.

Fred Trueman: Aye, it's a pity your mother didn't!

(After the ball Subba Row had dropped off Trueman's bowling had gone for four)

A Question Of Ethics

I never play cricket. It requires one to assume such indecent procedures.

Oscar Wilde

Close To The Edge

Admirers joked that he [J. T. Kellet-Kirtley] squatted with his face so close to the bails so that he could flick them off with his moustache.

Clive Crickmer

National Identity

My definition of a foreigner is someone who doesn't understand cricket.

Anthony Couch

Extra-Curricular Activities

What young men and young ladies get up to in the evenings during a Test Match doesn't worry me a bit.

Ted Dexter

Poseur

Posing with no clothes on does not do the game any good. There's far too much of that thing going on.

MCC Secretary Lt Col John Stephenson, after Chris Lewis bared all in a magazine

Logistics

If the best spin bowler in the country were a woman, what would be done about the dressing-room at Lord's?

Sir Neville Cardus

Let's Get Physical

To be a great bowler, you need a big heart and a big bottom.

Fred Trueman

In-laws and Outlaws
Pakistan is the sort of place every man should send his mother-in-law to, for a month, all expenses paid.
  Ian Botham

Come Dancing
Hostess: Aren't you going to dance, Mr [Arthur] Mailey?
Mailey: No Ma'am, I'm a little stiff from bowling.
Hostess: Oh really, so that's where you come from!

2. Media Watch

Time Out
Watching cricket is easy. All anyone needs is a deckchair, a pipe or knitting, and a week off from the office.
  Time Magazine

The Naked Truth
A freaker!
  John Arlott, commenting on the appearance of a streaker during a cricket match. He went on to add: 'Very shapely, and it's masculine. Fine performance, but what will they do about finding his swimming trunks?'

Against The Tide
Martin McCague will go down in history as the rat who joined the sinking ship.
  Sydney Telegraph

Denis the Menace
He [Norman Cowans] should remember what happened to Graham Dilley, who started off as a genuinely quick bowler. Then they started stuffing 'line and length' into his ear, and now he has Dennis Lillee's action with Denis Thatcher's pace.
  Geoff Boycott

Grace Before Meals
The Australian came down like a wolf on the fold,
The Mary'bone Cracks for a while were bowled;
Our Grace before dinner was very soon done,
And Our Grace after dinner did not get a run.
  Punch [1878]

Freedom Of Choice
I'm here to propose a toast to sportswriters and it's up to you if you stand up.

Fred Trueman, at a dinner engagement

Miracle at Trent Bridge
There has been a heavy fall of rain here at Trent Bridge; fortunately it didn't touch the ground.

BBC Radio Three announcer

Saying Something Stupid
He looks as if he's shitting . . . sitting on a shooting stick without the shooting stick.

Brian Johnston from Sporting Gaffes

Life Support Machines
We owe some gratitude to Gatting and Lamb, who breathed some life into a corpse which had nearly expired.

Trevor Bailey

Technical Assistance
Bill Frindall has done a bit of mental arithmetic with a calculator.

John Arlott

Escapism
Cricket is like sex films – they relieve frustration and tension.
Linda Lovelace

Newsflash
The latest news is that Warr's declared.
Brian Johnston, commentating on Middlesex v Sussex in 1939

Urgency
He [Ian Botham] plays a net as if he is on Weston-super-Mare beach and the tide is coming in fast.
Frank Keating

One Of A Kind?
This Centenary Lord's Test is a unique occasion – a repeat of Melbourne 1977.
Jim Laker

Advertising
I used to bowl tripe, then I wrote it, now I sell it.
Sign outside Arthur Mailey's butcher shop in Sydney

Fashion Statement
Dennis Lillee is wearing a voluminous nightshirt which would have room for another man, if he could get into the trousers.
John Arlott

Plodder

[Geoff] Boycott batted under the premise that 'slow and sure
wins the race'. His tactics for winning the Indy 500 would
have been to slip a council dust-cart into second gear.
   Colin M. Jarman

Close Contact!

The bowler's Holding, the batsman's Willey.
   Brian Johnston

Ashes To Ashes

Ashes to ashes, dust to dust
If Thomson don't get ya, Lillee must.
   Sydney Telegraph

3. Player Power

Not All He Seems

The face of a choirboy [Derek Underwood], the demeanour of
a civil servant and the ruthlessness of a rat-catcher.
   Geoff Boycott

Preamble

I don't go that far [as Bob Willis' run-up] on my holidays.
   Anon

Service

You have done for Australian cricket what the Boston
Strangler did for door-to-door salesmen.
   *Jack Birney to Geoff Boycott, after he had taken an eternity to
   score fifty at Perth*

Positive Thinking

At least I can catch up on some sleep. I've got about seven
years owing.
   *Ian Botham on his month-long stay in hospital for a
   back operation*

Modesty

If I could add your shots to my brain, I would be an
incredible player.
   Geoff Boycott to David Gower

Consuming Passions
I hadn't realised that it would be such an opportunity to invite the current England women's cricket team.
  Rachael Heyhoe-Flint after seeing a pack of pastry with directions 'Makes a pie for four people, or twelve little tarts'

Focus
Broken marriages, conflicts of loyalty, the problems of everyday life fall away as one faces up to [Jeff] Thomson.
  Mike Brearley

Poetry In Motion
Bonny Botham my oh me
Hit the ball at ten to three
Didn't come down 'til after tea.
  Jeff Cloves

Humility
Unless I'm crackers or something, I've scored a bloody sight more runs than that bearded old bugger.
  Geoff Boycott on W. G. Grace

Economy
It's hard work making batting look effortless.
  David Gower

Attack Is The Best Form Of Defence
I don't like defensive shots, you can only get threes.
  W. G. Grace

Mitigating Circumstances
It's the ground; it's too far away.
  W. G. Grace, after missing a ball in the outfield

Rabbiting On
We used to eat so many salads, there was a danger of contracting myxomatosis.
  Ray East

Spoilsport
He [Donald Bradman] spoilt the game – he got too many runs.
  Jack Hobbs

Terminal Illness
It's difficult to be more laid back without being actually comatose.
Frances Edmonds on David Gower

Primitive
A dry fart!
Phil Edmonds, on being asked what he looked forward to most upon returning from a long tour of India

Understatement
He [Ian Botham] would probably not fit the bill as the schoolboy's vision of the dedicated superstar.
Graham Gooch

The Sting In The Tale
Yes, he's a very good cricketer – pity he's not a better batter or bowler.
Tom Graveney

The Drinking Classes
If the crowd throw bottles at us, we'll hurl 'em straight back – unless they are full, of course.
Rachael Heyhoe-Flint

Might-have-been
If my mother hadn't thrown my football boots on the fire, I might have become as famous as Denis Compton.
Sir Len Hutton

Not Guilty
I don't try to be Joe Blow, the super stud – it just happens.
Jeff Thomson

Sacrifice
Ken Barrington [during a mid-wicket conference in a Test match]: Let's cut out some of the quick singles.
Fred Titmus: OK! We'll cut out yours, Ken!

Idol Worship
I didn't get Bradman's autograph, but he trod on my toe, though.
Anon

Geography Lesson
There's only one head bigger than Tony Greig's, and that's Birkenhead.
Fred Trueman

Mystery Man
Geoff Boycott is enough of an enigma to puzzle the sphinx.
David Gower

Diminished Capacity
[Glenn] Turner looks a bit shaky and unsteady, but I think he's going to bat on – one ball left!
Brian Johnston, after Turner sustained a painful blow to his reproductive organs

Amazing Grace
Had Grace been born in ancient Greece, *the Iliad* would have been a different book.
The Bishop of Hereford

4. Coaching and Tactics

Fortune-teller
No captain with all the hindsight in the world can predict how the wicket is going to play.
Trevor Bailey

Obsolescent
England's pace bowlers are making the helmet go out of fashion.
Scyld Berry

Accidents Will Happen
If I ever bowled a maiden over, it's not my fault.
Arthur Mailey

Minimalism
I wouldn't say I coached him, but I didn't mess him up.
Coach George Fenner, on Denis Compton

False Expectation
When's the game itself going to begin?
Groucho Marx, on seeing his first cricket match

Heavenly Misadventure

You might keep your eyes shut when you're praying, Vicar, but I wish you'd keep 'em open when I'm bowling.

Fred Trueman, after the Rev David Sheppard had dropped a catch off his bowling in the slips·

The Heart Of The Matter

The great skill in modern cricket is getting a side out that wants to stay in.

Tony Brown

A Rule Of Thumb

You should play every game as if it's your last, but make sure you perform well enough to ensure it's not.

John Emburey

Projection

What do they expect me to do? Walk around in a T-shirt with 'I'm in charge' on it?

David Gower, on reports that the English selectors were unhappy with his laid-back style of captaincy

From Bad To Worse

He's doing the best he can do – he's making the worst of a bad job.

Fred Trueman

Batty
When you win the toss – bat.
If you are in doubt, think about it – then bat.
If you have very big doubts, consult a colleague – then bat.
  W.G. Grace

King Arthur
If that chap in the brown Derby hat at the back of the grandstand had held his catches, I'd have had them out days ago.
  Arthur Mailey (after figures of 64-0-362-4, when Victoria scored a record 1,107 runs in 1926)

On The Same Game
Very few chances were given, but I think a chap in a tweed coat dropped Jack Ryder [295] near the shilling stand.

P. S.
It was rather a pity that Ellis got out at 1,107, because I was just striking a length.

Sexism
Professional coaching is a man trying to get you to keep your legs together when other men have spent a lifetime trying to get them wide apart.
  Rachael Heyhoe-Flint

Unpredictable
Pitches are like wives, you can never tell how they're going to turn out.
  Sir Len Hutton

Uninviting
As harrowing experiences go, there can't be much to choose between the Australian cricket captaincy and social work on Skid Row.
  Doug Ibbotson

5. Umpires

A Hybrid
There's no more amateurish professional game in the world.
  John Emburey

Disability

When a cricketer no longer had nerve, eye or sinew left, then he was put out to grass as an umpire.

Robert A. Fitzgerald

Box-office Draw

They haven't come to see you umpiring, they have come to see me bat.

W. G. Grace, on being given out lbw and refusing to walk

Wanted

A cricket umpire should be above all suspicion of bias, and free from all odours of the tavern.

Rachael Heyhoe-Flint

Victim

Most of the time he [an umpire] stands to be shot at;
An immobile creature, for mankind to pot at.

Alec Skelding

Logical

I cannot for the life of me see why the umpires, the only two people on a cricket field who are not going to get grass stains on their knees, are the only two people allowed to wear dark trousers.

Katherine Whitehorn

Getting Their Teeth Into It

It is rather suitable for umpires to dress like dentists, since one of their tasks is to draw stumps.

John Arlott

Sex Discrimination

An umpire should be a man. They are for the most part old women.

Robert A. Fitzgerald

6. A Cricket Stew

Bliss

Cricket is indescribable. How do you describe an orgasm?

Greg Matthews

I.Q.
Spinning – it's all a matter of inches; those between your ears.
  Arthur Milton

Awareness
Are you aware, [Dennis Lillee] Sir, that the last time I saw
anything like that on a top-lip, the whole herd had to
be destroyed?
  Eric Morecambe, referring to 'foot and mouth' disease

Food For Thought
Boycott, somewhat a creature of habit, likes exactly the sort of
food he himself prefers.
  Don Mosey

Incompatible
I am to cricket what Dame Sybil Thorndyke is to
non-ferrous welding.
  Frank Muir

Mistaken Identity
Friend: What do you think of the Test?
George Bernard Shaw: What are they testing?

As It Nearly Said In The Bible
I am not my brother's wicket-keeper.
  Clyde Packer

Consenting Adults
Women playing cricket should treat it as a matter between
playing consenting females in private.
  Michael Parkinson

On Your Toes
A wicket-keeper who is on his toes is likely to overbalance.
  C. B. Ponsonby

The Artful Dodger
When we first got married, Derek used to throw tea cups
behind his back and catch them. That's one way he got out
of doing the washing-up.
  Liz Randall

Rivalry

I enjoy the way the Australians play their cricket, but they could be a bit more gracious. Being called a f***ing c**t to your face is a bit much.

England cricketer Phil Tufnell

Lazy

Personally, I have always looked on cricket as organised loafing.

William Temple

First Come . . .

Everyone knows which comes first when it's a question of cricket or sex – all discerning people recognise that.

Harold Pinter

Gaffe

Yorkshire were 232 all out, Hutton ill. No! I'm sorry, Hutton 111.

John Snagge – radio commentator

Side By Side

Dying man's request: Bury me 20 yards from Fred, so I can send him a ball, once in a blue moon.

Anon [In fact, they were buried 25 yards apart to allow for a run-up]

Wine, Women and Song
If I'd done a quarter of the things of which I'm accused, I'd be pickled with alcohol. I'd be a registered drug addict and would have sired half the children in most of the world's cricket-playing countries.
Ian Botham

Useless
He [Ian Botham] couldn't bowl a hoop downhill.
Fred Trueman

Touring Party
Done the elephants, done the poverty, nothing left to do.
Phil Tufnell, after a few days of the tour to India

Foreign Exchange
When you come back from touring Australia, you almost feel like you've been to Vietnam.
Glenn Turner

The Origin of the Species
I have always imagined cricket as a game invented by roughnecks in a moment of idleness by casually throwing an unexploded bomb at one another. The game was observed by some officer with a twisted and ingenious mind who devoted his life to inventing impossible rules for it.
Peter Ustinov

Comparison
Cricket is baseball on valium.
Robin Williams

Safety
A young boy's parents were getting divorced.
Judge: Would you like to live with your father?
Boy: No, he beats me.
Judge: So you would like to live with your mother?
Boy: No, she beats me.
Judge: Well, who would you like to live with?
Boy: The English cricket team – they can't beat anyone!

8

Football's Fun and Frolics

Football's belly-button is liberally sprinkled with bootroom banter, boardroom battles, thrilling tricksters and walls of waffle. In this environment some comments from football personalities are meant to amuse, and others are meant to enlighten. As we shall see, many of the funniest football quotations fall into the second category! The following collection is a distillation of gems from the players and managers of the past and present. In addition you will find writers, household names, neglected talents, the odd indefinable genius and perhaps some new voices. Everything you ever wanted to know about football will not be here – but the contents prove conclusively that for wit, originality and generally great laughs, it really is 'a funny old game'.

1. The Managerial Merry-Go-Round

The Work Ethic
A lot of hard work went into this defeat.
Malcolm Allison

Unimpressive
He [Graham Taylor] is as useless as a back pocket in a vest.
Anon

Really Minty
I think Ally MacLeod [Scotland's manager in 1978] believes
tactics are a new kind of peppermint.
Anon Scottish international

Coaching
I went down to pass on some technical information to the
team – like the fact the game had started.
*Ron Atkinson, explaining why he had taken his seat in the
dugout earlier than normal in Aston Villa's 0-1 home defeat
against lowly Sheffield United*

Belief
I'm not a believer in luck, although I do believe you need it.
Alan Ball (whose autobiography is entitled It's All About a Ball*)*

Confident Prediction
I honestly believe that we can go all the way to
Wembley…unless somebody knocks us out.
Dave Bassett

In The Name Of The Father
Gordon Lee: Well, what business has anyone got naming him
Eamon O'Keefe if he isn't Irish?
Billy Bingham: Probably the same business they have naming
you Lee when you're not Chinese!

Always Look On The Bright Side Of Life
Matt (Busby) always believed Manchester United would be
one of the greatest clubs in the world. He was the eternal
optimist. In 1968 he still hoped Glenn Miller was just missing.
Pat Crerand

Nice Legs, Shame About The Face
His face is in such a mess I'm going to bring him home and put him on the mantelpiece to keep the kids away from the fire.
Dundalk manager Dermot Keeley, after an injury to one of his players

My Word Is My Bond
I promise results, not promises.
John Bond

If Only
The game in Romania was a game we should have won. We lost it because we thought we were going to win it. But then again, I thought there was no way we were going to get a result there.
Slightly muddled Jack Charlton, after Ireland's defeat by Bulgaria in 1987

Plain Speaking
Tommy Docherty: An absolute disgrace, that's what you [Stewart Houston] are! A dis-frigging-grace to that red shirt you're wearing. In that first half, you were S.H.I.T. And that spells shit, son!
Lou Macari: Don't beat about the bush, boss. Just tell him how you really think he's been playing.

Watch Your Back
He [Aston Villa chairman Doug Ellis] said he was right behind me, so I told him I'd rather have him in front where I could see him.
Tommy Docherty

Quote Of The Year
The man from Del Monte said 'Yes'.
Telegram sent to the holidaying Roy Evans, to tell him that Stan Collymore had signed for Liverpool

I'm Not Looking For Excuses, But . . .
The first thing that went wrong was half-time. We could have done without that.
Graham Taylor, explaining England's second half collapse against Sweden in the European Championships in 1992

Earth Shattering
In terms of the Richter scale, this defeat was a force 8 gale.
John Lyall

River Deep And Mountain High
He's my man mountain – he would head aeroplanes away if
it helped Birmingham City.
Barry Fry, on Liam Daish

Resignation Issue
He [Graham Taylor] should leave the same way he arrived.
Fired with enthusiasm.
Joe Lovejoy

Suicide
There's never a good time to score an own goal against yourself.
John Greig

All I Need Is The Air That I Breathe
The air conditioning was good.
*Norwegian agent Rune Hauge's response to journalists after
giving evidence at the George Graham 'bung' tribunal*

True Grit
Very few players have the courage of my convictions.
Brian Clough

New Identity

Tell him he's Pele.

Partick Thistle manager John Lambie after being told that his striker, Colin McGlashan, had a head injury and didn't know who he was

Memorial

The last player to score a hat-trick in an FA Cup Final was Stan Mortensen. He even had a Final named after him – The Matthews Final.

Lawrie McMenemy

Tough Talking

Now listen, boys, I'm not happy with our tackling. We're hurting them, but they keep getting up.

Jimmy Murphy

Call-up

Mike Smith: Hi, Vinny. I'm the manager of Wales, and we'd like you to play for us. You do like Wales, Vinny?
Vinny Jones: Of course I do, I've seen Moby Dick twice!

Attributed but apocryphal

Hard Times

Mind, I've been here during the bad times too. One year we came second.

Bob Paisley

Two Out Of Three Ain't Bad

I like defenders to be big, mean and ugly. Two out of three ain't bad. Are you mean as well?

Former Irish international Ray Treacy, to defender Peter Eccles, after his appointment as manager of Shamrock Rovers

All Kinds Of Balls

I do want to play the long ball, and I do want to play the short ball. I think long and short balls is what football is all about.

Bobby Robson

Yell For Tel

Certain people are for me, certain people are pro me.

Terry Venables

Wipe Out

I'm going to tape *Neighbours* over this.
West Ham boss Harry Redknapp, on receiving the video recording of his side's goalless draw with Southampton

Team Spirit

Before the match, I told my players they will be playing against 11 (Blackburn) guys ready to fight for each other for 90 minutes . . . but I didn't expect it to be *with* each other!
Spartak Moscow coach Oleg Romantsev, after the infamous brawl involving Blackburn's Graeme Le Saux and David Batty

Selection Policy

I don't drop players – I make changes.
Bill Shankly

Questions and Answers

During Brian Clough's Derby days, he rang down to the dressing-room for a cup of tea. The apprentice who answered said simply: 'Bugger off', and slammed down the phone. Clough rang down again, asking: 'Do you know who I am?' The apprentice answered with another question: 'Do you know who I am?'
'No.'
'Well, bugger off again, then.'

2. Love and Marriage

Predictability

Like sex, the movements in football are limited and predictable.
Peter Ackroyd

Slander

John Bond has blackened my name with his insinuations about the private lives of football managers. Both my wives are upset.
Malcolm Allison

Afterlife

If I come back in the next life, I want to come back as George Best's fingertips.
Anon

Seen But Not Heard

Women should be in the kitchen, the discotheque and the boutique, but not in football.

Ron Atkinson

True Love

That was very considerate of you. [Man United fan on the way to Old Trafford seeing a colleague getting on his knees as a funeral cortege passed by.]

It's the least I could do. I was married to her for fifty years.

The Discerning Eye

If you want the secret of my success with women, then don't smoke, don't take drugs and don't be too particular.

George Best

Fan

I'd rather have a guy take me to a football match and have a drink afterwards than go to bed with someone.

Samantha Fox

Odds On

If I had a choice of a night with Raquel Welch or going to a betting shop, I'd choose the betting shop.

Stan Bowles

Witch Hunt

With our luck, one of our players must be bonking a witch.

Ken Brown (ex-Norwich manager)

Simply Red

Staff member at Old Trafford in the sixties: I have terrible news for you.

Alarmed colleague: What?

Staff member: I'm afraid your wife is having an affair.

Alarmed colleague: Is that all? I thought you were going to tell me that George Best was injured!

Put Down

The biggest waste of money since Madonna's father bought her a pair of pyjamas.

Celtic fan's verdict on Tony Cascarino

Bonnie Prince Charlie

We talked about football, but really all he [Charlie Nicholas]
wanted to talk about was sex…I hear he's not been
scoring many goals recently and that's why he left Arsenal,
but all I can tell you is, he certainly scored a hat-trick with me
that night.

*Therese Bazar, ex-singer with the hit-making band of the
seventies, Dollar*

Golden Years

I'm ill-tempered, rude and wondering what's for tea; just the
same as always.

*Brian Clough, on what he is like at 4.40 pm on a Saturday
afternoon since his retirement*

Women's Lib

Women run everything. The only thing that I have done
within my house in the last 20 years is to recognise Angola as
an independent state.

Brian Clough

In Stitches

Tony Dunne: How's the mouth?
Bill Foulkes [with four stitches in his mouth]: She's at home with
the kids.

True Love
I love Liverpool so much that if I caught one of their players in bed with my missus, I'd tiptoe downstairs and make him a cup of tea.

A Koppite

Do You Think I'm Sexy?
If Rod Stewart can't pull the best-looking girls in the world, what chance do the rest of us have?

Mo Johnston

Helpful Hint
Taxi-driver: How about a tip?
Irish fan at 1994 World Cup: Why, certainly. Use a deodorant and get to meet more girls.

Birthday Suit
Nurse: Take off your clothes and I will examine you in a minute.
George Best: Where will I leave them?
Nurse: On top of mine. [She had returned totally naked!]

Hung(a)ry Lips
I got so many kisses after this goal that they would have sufficed a modest woman for a lifetime.

*Ferenc Puskas, after scoring for Hungary in the 1952
Olympic Final*

Love Story
Of course I didn't take my wife to see Rochdale as an anniversary present. It was her birthday. Would I have got married during the football season? And, anyway, it wasn't Rochdale, it was Rochdale reserves.

Bill Shankly

On Hold
To suggest a player shouldn't have sex the night before a match is the height of silliness. I've had enjoyable nights and mornings before a game and it never affected me. But before a match I won't put a lot of energy into it.

Graeme Souness

Stimulus Variation
The orgies, the birds and the fabulous money – football is just a distraction.

Peter Storey, ex-Arsenal star

Foreplay
It's not the sex that tires out young footballers, it's staying up half the night looking for it.

Clemens Westerhof, coach of Nigeria in US '94

3. Fan-tasy

Dedication
A fan is one who knows the true nationality of every player who plays for Ireland.

Anon

Luck
We beat them five-nothing, and they were lucky to score nothing.

Anon

The Not So Mighty Quinn
Quinn, you're rubbish. In fact, you're so bad, I could keep the ball off you for 90 minutes – in a telephone box.

Arsenal fan to Niall Quinn, when he was an Arsenal player and his own fans refused to give him the ball back after it went out for a throw-in at Highbury

Final Score
Three-nil already! What's it up to?

Young boy, attending his first game, after his father's side had gone three-up after five minutes

Fruit and Veg
Some fruit and vegetable dealers did very well.

John Barnes, after Everton fans greeted him with bananas

What's In A Name?
I call the Irish Prime Minister 'Tea-shop' because I can't pronounce his name properly.

Jack Charlton

Razor Sharp
TOMMY COYNE. SHARPER THAN JIMMY HILL'S CHIN.
Banner at Ireland v Italy

Euthanasia
The ideal board of directors should be made up of three men
– two dead and one dying.
Tommy Docherty

By Hooks Or By Crooks
Maggie [Thatcher] isn't the only one with Crooks at No. 11.
Spurs fans' banner, 1981

Logic
If you can't join them, beat them!
*Government minister, after Denmark's European Championships
triumph in 1992, following their rejection of the Maastricht Treaty*

Changing Tastes
I used to play football for Scotland until I discovered Smirnoff.
Graffiti

Vandalism
Football hooligans? Well, there are ninety-two club chairmen,
for a start.
Brian Clough

La Fin
Eric Cantona has given up football. He's just signed for Arsenal.
Graffiti

Scot's Gallic
What would Scotland be like without football? English.
Tony Higgins

A Fishy Story
Jack Charlton once caught a fish so big that after he landed it, the level of the lake fell by ten feet.
Irish fan

Wired For Sound
Excuse me, but do Irish people not have televisions in their homes?
American tourist, in a packed hotel during an Ireland-Norway game

Forgive and Forget
A fan is a person who, when you have made an idiot of yourself on the pitch, doesn't think you've done a permanent job.
Francis Lee

Direction
Princess Margaret: But Mr Labone, where is Everton?
Brian Labone: In Liverpool, Ma'am.
HRH: Of course, we had your first team here last year.
Bill Shankly's version of the 1966 FA Cup Final

Thuggery
If Rugby Football was a hooligan's game played by gentlemen, then Association was a gentlemen's game not only played by hooligans but also watched by them.
Tony Masson

Freedom Of Choice
Many supporters say they wouldn't stand for all-seater stadiums.
Guy Michelmore

Good Advice?
Remember, postcards only, please. The winner will be the first one opened.
Brian Moore

A True Fan
I shall continue to give relegated Luton my full support – in fact, I'm wearing it at this very moment.
Eric Morecambe

Striking A Positive Note
Yes, the band.
The Queen, when asked if anyone had played well in a poor Cup Final

The First Cut's The Deepest
David May Models New Team Strip [caption under photograph showing plump, elderly nun kicking a football]
Manchester United fanzine Red Attitude

Beyond Pessimism
Pessimists see a cup that is half-empty. Optimists see a cup that is half-full. But we [QPR fans] haven't even seen the cup.
QPR fanzine

Pride and Prejudice
I object to you even suggesting that I'm a bigot just because I say I hate Celtic with a passion.
Rangers supporter

Tops Of The Bottoms
It's tight, taut and muscular. Bobby Moore's posterior comes top of our Girls' Bottom League.
John Samuel, journalist

The Long Arm Of The Law
Q: What do Manchester United and O.J. Simpson have in common?
A: They both get away with murder at home!

Two Of A Kind
Two Gary Stevens; there's only two Gary Stevens.
English fans' chant at 1986 World Cup, when Gary Stevens
[Spurs] and Gary Stevens [Everton] played together for England

All Preachers Great And Small
Football causeth fighting, brawling, contention, quarrel-
picking, murder, homicide, and a great effusion of blood, as
daily experiences teaches.
Phillip Stubbes, 1583

Pithy
Fan [after Blackburn lost a crucial match]: Kenny, can I have a
quick word?
Kenny Dalglish [attributed]: Velocity.

Girls and Boys
Football is all very well as a game for rough girls, but it is
hardly suitable for delicate boys.
Oscar Wilde

4. Media Matters

Amateur v Professional
A lot of people in football don't have much time for the press;
they say they're amateurs. But I say to those people, 'Noah
was an amateur, but the Titanic was built by professionals.'
Malcolm Allison

Last Resort
They must go for it now as they have nothing to lose but
the match.
Ron Atkinson

New Custom
As recently as the late Seventies, to woo our top players
home, the authorities introduced all-day drinking in Scottish
pubs; a valiant effort that succeeded only in enticing George
Best to Hibs.
BBC Radio Scotland

Expert Comment

John Motson: Well, Trevor, what does this substitution mean, tactically?

Trevor Brooking: Well, Barnes has come off and Rocastle has come on . . .

Prince Charmingless

Kenny Dalglish has about as much personality as a tennis racket.

Mick Channon

The Winner Takes It All?

If in winning the game we only finish with a draw, we would be fine.

Jack Charlton

Analysis

Nottingham Forest are having a bad run . . . they've lost six matches now without winning.

David Coleman

Lethal

Trevor Brooking floats like a butterfly, and stings like one too.

Brian Clough

Punditry
There was a problem of balance, but it was the same for both sides.
George Curtis

Expert Insight
You know, the Brazilians aren't as good as they used to be, or as they are now.
Kenny Dalglish

Jeepers Keepers
Lukic saved with his foot which is all part of the goalkeeper's arm.
Barry Davies

Impotence
He [Ray Wilkins] can't run, he can't tackle and he can't head the ball. The only time he goes forward is to toss the coin.
Tommy Docherty

Back To School
Conjugate the verb 'done great': I done great. He done great. We done great. They done great. The boy Lineker done great.
Letter to The Guardian *on Channon and Emlyn Hughes' performance as World Cup pundits*

Fightback
Hearts 2 Motherwell 0. A good fightback there by Motherwell, who were 2-0 down at one stage.
Paddy Feeney

There's Lies, Damned Lies and Statistics
Up to five goals is journalism; after that, it becomes statistics.
Emmanuel Gambardella, journalist, after Sweden defeated Cuba 8-0

It's A Funny Old Game
He hit the post, and after the game people will say, well, he hit the post.
Jimmy Greaves

Clueless
Poor Fulham, with no real method up front, resembled a fire engine hurrying to the wrong fire.
Geoffrey Green

Curious
The game finely balanced, with Celtic well on top.
John Greig

National Geographic
If a week's a long time in politics, it is an equinox in football.
Stuart Hall

If You Can't Stand The Heat . . . .
It's 110 degrees and it has to be said that it's well over 100.
George Hamilton

Clear And Present Danger
The USA are a goal down, and if they don't get a goal, they'll lose.
John Helm

Chapter and Verse
Interviewer: You've devoted a whole chapter of your book to Jimmy Greaves.
Pat Jennings: That's right. Well, what can you say about Jimmy Greaves?

All Creatures Great And Small
Sporting Lisbon in their green and white hoops, looking like a team of zebras.
Peter Jones

Let's Be Frank
Sport, let's be honest, doesn't really matter. Over the years we have had General Elections won or lost by the Poor Laws, the Corn Laws, never the Denis Laws.
Frank Keating

Every Face Tells A Story
His [Bobby Robson] natural expression is that of a man who fears he might have left the gas on.
David Lacey

Tactical Suggestion
Bobby Robson must be thinking of throwing some fresh legs on.
  Kevin Keegan

Stating the Obvious
Dickie Davies: What's he going to be telling his team at half-time, Denis?
Denis Law: He'll be telling them that there are forty-five minutes left to play.

Cheat
Hodge scored for Forest after only twenty-two seconds, totally against the run of play.
  Peter Lorenzo

David and Goliath
England were losing to a mountain top. Ben Nevis 1, the Turnips 0.
  Joe Lovejoy, on England's 1993 World Cup qualifier against San Marino

Derby Game
Chesterfield 1, Chester 1. Another score draw there in that local derby.
  Desmond Lynam

On Ramsey Street
Are you [a journalist at a Press Conference during the 1994
World Cup] from Australia? What's happening in *Neighbours*?
    Jason McAteer

Briefs Encounter
[Liam] Brady's been playing inside Platini's shorts all night.
    RTE commentator Jimmy Magee

The Heat Is On
The news from Guadalajara, where the temperature is 96
degrees, is that Falcao is warming up.
    Brian Moore

Unequal Balance
The game is balanced in Arsenal's favour.
    John Motson

The Vikings
Lord Nelson . . Sir Winston Churchill . . Lady Diana . .
Maggie Thatcher, can you hear me? Your boys took a hell of
a beating!
    *Norwegian commentator, after Norway's shock victory over
    England in a World Cup qualifier in 1981*

Incredible
With the very last kick of the game, Bobby McDonald scored
with a header.
    Alan Parry

Comprehensive
The first ninety minutes are the most important.
    Bobby Robson

Bargain Basement
The InterTwobob Cup.
    The Sun on the Intertoto Cup

Passover
If Stan [Bowles] could pass a betting shop like he can pass a
ball, he'd have no worries at all.
    Ernie Tagg, on the ex-international's gambling compulsion

Action Replay
Arsenal, Wednesday, Thursday.

The Sunday Times' headline announcing the replay date after Arsenal and Sheffield Wednesday drew in the 1993 FA Cup Final

Reporting
Swedes 2, Turnips 1

The Sun's headline after Sweden's win over England in 1992

Advice
This is a goal, this is a ball. Put one in the other and advance.

The Daily Mirror's advice to the English soccer team

Desperation
Graham Taylor has been arrested in America for shaking a cigarette machine, but the cops let him off when he said he only wanted to borrow 20 Players.

Irish comedienne Maureen Potter, after America's shock defeat of England in 1993

Perspective
Yanks 2 Planks 0

The Sun after England lost that same match

Reporting
Norse Manure

The Daily Mirror's verdict after Norway beat England

Fools Rush In
If there's a goal now, I'll eat my hat!

BBC radio commentator Tommy Woodruffe during the 1938 FA Cup Final. There was, and he did!

A Simple Game, Really
The rules of soccer are basically simple – if it moves, kick it; if it doesn't move, kick it until it does.

Phil Woosnam

The Second Time Around
If history is going to repeat itself, I should think we can expect the same thing again.

Terry Venables

5. Holy Wit

Precision
I hear Glenn Hoddle has found God [after Hoddle
became a born-again Christian]. That must have been one hell
of a pass!
  Jasper Carrott

Saint Jack?
Reporter: Jack, the Irish people will probably canonise you
after what you've achieved in the World Cup in Italy.
Jack Charlton: Canonisation? You couldn't do that to me – I'm
a Protestant!

Saints Alive
Poster on wall: What would you do if Jesus returned among us?
Graffiti: Move St John to inside left!

Suspicious Mind
*Mrs Cohen [her son had just become the first Israeli international
to play for Liverpool]:* Do you still wear your skull cap?
Avi: No one wears skull caps in Liverpool.
Mrs Cohen: Do you still go to the synagogue on the Sabbath?
Avi: How can I? We have a match every Saturday.
Mrs Cohen [attributed]: Tell me, are you still circumcised?

Funeral Arrangements
He's [fellow coach] not so much a coach as a hearse.
  Tommy Docherty

Religious Advertising
Jesus saves – but Keegan scores on the rebound.
  Graffiti

The Gospel Truth
Last time we got a penalty away from home, Christ was still
a carpenter.
  Lenny Lawrence

The Singing Nun
He [Kevin Keegan] is the Julie Andrews of football.
  Duncan McKenzie

The Dark Ages
We've got grounds which are state of the art and administration which is state of the Ark.
Gordon Taylor (of the PFA), criticising the investigation into the 'bung scandal'

Hedging Your Bets
I'm not superstitious or anything like that, but I'll just hope that we'll play our best and put it in the lap of the Gods.
Terry Neill

6. Foreign Affairs

The French Connection
Martin Buchan: From its style, it [George Best's coat] looks French.
George Best: It is from France. It's Toulon and Toulouse!

The Important Things Of Life
My only problem [after his transfer to Italy] seems to be with Italian breakfasts. No matter how much money you've got, you can't get any Rice Krispies.
Luther Blissett

Don't Know Much About Geography
We fought two wars with the Germans. We probably got on better with the smaller nations like the Dutch, the Belgians, the Norwegians and the Swedes, some of whom are not even in Europe.
Jack Charlton

Out Of Africa
If the African nations ever succeeded in their plan for one British team in the World Cup, I'd vote Tory. That is how serious it is. I ask you, a load of spear throwers trying to dictate our role in world football.
Brian Clough

In The Boardroom
There's a hell of a lot of politics in football. I don't think Henry Kissinger would have lasted 48 hours at Old Trafford.
Tommy Docherty

Change Of Heart
The doctor at Lazio told me I should try drinking wine, because it would be good for me. When I did, he had one look at me and said: 'You'd better go back on the beer.'
Gazza

Surprise, Surprise
Well, stone me. We've had cocaine, bribery and Arsenal scoring two goals at home. But just when you thought there truly were no surprises left in football, Vinnie Jones turns out to be an international player.
Jimmy Greaves

Solid Gold?
The European Cup is seventeen pounds of silver and it's worth its weight in gold.
Brian Moore

Psychological Warfare
I'm not giving away any secrets like that to Milan. If I had my way, I wouldn't even tell them the time of the kick-off.
Bill Shankly, on the delayed announcement of his team line-up before a European game

Revelation
The World Cup – truly an international event.
  John Motson

Off-the-Wall
I have Gary Lineker's shirt up in my hotel room, and it's only stopped moving now.
  Mick McCarthy, the day after Ireland's win against England in 1988

Star Performer
With Maradona, even Arsenal would have won it [the 1986 World Cup].
  Bobby Robson

Fancy That
Moving from Wales to Italy is like going to a different country.
  Ian Rush

9

Golfing Gems

To the outsider, golf is a bizarre sport created by God on a bad day to pay humankind back for all its crimes. To the devotee, it is an obsession. Just ask any of those most pathetic of creatures, the 'golf widow' or 'golf widower'! Inspiring as it does such extremes of love and hate, golf is the ideal breeding ground for memorable quotations. The following collection will do nothing to improve your game nor eradicate your prejudice as the case may be, but it will make you laugh. Wherever you stand on the great golf divide, these quotations remind you in the immortal words of Gerry and the Pacemakers that 'you'll never walk alone'.

1. What's the Name of the Game?

Tragi-comedy
Amateur: 'Golf's a funny old game.'
Scottish caddy: 'It's no' intended to be funny, and the way you play it, it's downright tragic.'

Fandom
A golf ball is a small object that remains on the tee while a perspiring citizen fans it vigorously with a large club.
   Peter Andrews

The Numbers Game
The true definition of a golfer is one who shouts 'Fore', takes five, and puts down a three.
   Anon

Definition
Golf – hockey at the halt.
   Anon

Advantage
Golf is a lot of walking, broken up by disappointment and bad arithmetic.
   Paul Aston

Pun
Jack on my Back
   Title of Jack Nicklaus' caddy Andrea Angela's book

Grace
Golf is an awkward set of bodily contortions designed to produce a graceful result.
Tommy Armour

Mixed Motive
It's not in support of cricket, but as an earnest protest against golf.
Sir Max Beerbohm, on giving a shilling to W. G. Grace's testimonial

First Choice
Give me my golf clubs, fresh air and a beautiful partner, and you can keep my golf clubs and the fresh air.
Jack Benny

Profanity
The number of shots taken by an opponent who is out of sight is equal to the square root of the sum of the number of curses heard plus the number of swishes.
Michael Green

Irresistible
Golf is like the eighteen-year-old girl with the big boobs. You know it's wrong, but you can't keep away from her.
Val Doonican

Spelling
Have you ever noticed what golf spells backwards?
Al Boliska

Politically Incorrect
[Golf] An ineffectual attempt to direct an uncontrollable sphere into an inaccessible hole with instruments ill-adapted to the purpose.
Winston Churchill

Little and Large
Golf is a game in which a ball – one and a half inches in diameter – is placed on a ball – 8,000 miles in diameter. The object being to hit the small ball, but not the larger.
John Cunningham

Life Expectancy
There are two things that don't last long – dogs that chase cars and pros that putt for pars.
Lee Trevino

Agriculture
Golf is 'Cow-pasture pool'.
O.K. Bovard

No Win Situation
Golf is like a love affair: if you don't take it seriously, it's no fun; if you do take it seriously, it breaks your heart.
Arnold Daly

A Grave Matter
Golf is not a funeral, though both can be very sad affairs.
Bernard Darwin

The Pleasure Principle
Golf and sex are the only two things you can enjoy without being good at it.
Jimmy Demaret

Pastime
Golf is an ideal diversion, but a ruinous disease.
B. C. Forbes

Prevention Is Better Than Cure
In golf, as in medicine . . . the best way to get out of trouble is to avoid it.
Richard Gordon

Statistics
Ninety-five per cent of putts which finish short don't go in.
Hubert Green

Perfectionist Streak
Golf is the only game where the worst player gets the best of it. He obtains more out of it as regards both exercise and enjoyment, for the good player gets worried over the slightest mistake, whereas the poor player makes too many mistakes to worry over them.
David Lloyd George

Definition Of Terms

They call it golf because all the other four letter words
were taken.
  Walter Hagen

Terminal Three

That's what I call an airport shot. You hit one of those, you
miss the cut and you're heading off for the airport.
  Lee Trevino

Substance Abuse

Golf is the only sport where the players aren't penalised for
being on grass.
  Bob Hope

Best Of Both Worlds

[Golf] A game in which you claim the privileges of age, and
retain the playthings of childhood.
  Samuel Johnson

Retirement Plan

Golf is a game to be played between rugby and death.
  Nigel Pearce

No Fun

'Golf', he replied, 'was much too serious a matter to be
called a sport.'
  John Pearson in James Bond: The Authorised Biography
  of 007

Leisure

Golf is a good walk spoiled.
  Mark Twain

Occupational Therapy

Golf is a day spent in a round of strenuous idleness.
  William Wordsworth

Work Ethic

If you watch a game, it's fun. If you play it, it's recreation. If
you work at it, it's golf.
  Bob Hope

Travellers' Checks
Golf is merely an expensive way of leaving home.
Michael Parkinson

2. Style and Etiquette

The Clothes Show
[Paul] Azinger is wearing an all-black outfit – black jumper, blue trousers, white shoes, and a pink tea cosy.
Renton Laidlaw

A Load Of Bull
The core of the golf ball shall consist of a bull's penis, first prepared by skimming and drying.
W. Langstaff

Protocol
It's good sportsmanship to not pick up lost golf balls while they are still rolling.
Laurence J. Peter

Prior Warning
I always know which side a putt will break, it slopes towards the side of the green Herman [Mitchell, his heavyweight caddy] is standing.
Lee Trevino

Women's Lib
Mrs Elspeth Mustard [secretary to the Secretary at Muirfield, Edinburgh] to an American woman visitor: 'I am sorry, we don't allow ladies in the clubhouse.'
American woman: 'Then, what are you?'

Take Off
I just loosen my girdle and let 'er rip.
> *Mildred 'Babe' Zaharias on her driving style*

Keep Holy The Sabbath Day
God won't stop me entering the Kingdom of Heaven just because I play sport on Sunday.
> *Gary Player*

Dress Sense
I think those golfers who look as though they got dressed in the dark should be penalised two strokes each for offending the public eye.
> *Doug Sanders*

Simplicity
[Arnold] Palmer hitched up his baggy pants and turned golf into a game of 'Hit it hard, go find it and hit it hard again.'
> *John Schulian*

Distractions
I wish they would start talking about the quality of my golf, not my wardrobe; print my score, not my measurements.
> *Craig 'The Walrus' Stadler*

A Natural Law
The uglier a man's legs are, the better he plays golf. It's almost a law.
> *H.G. Wells*

Wardrobe
My golf swing is like ironing a shirt. You get one side smoothed out, turn it over and there is a big wrinkle on the other side. You iron that side, turn it over and there's another wrinkle.
> *Tom Watson*

Tight Fit
My backswing off the first tee had put him in mind of an elderly woman of dubious morals trying to struggle out of a dress too tight around the shoulders.
Patrick Campbell

All Creatures Great And Small
They say I'm famous for my delicate chip shots. Sure, when I hit them right, they land, just so, like a butterfly with sore feet.
Lee Trevino

Dress Sense
Golf is a game where white men can dress up as black pimps and get away with it.
Robin Williams

A Mother's Love
Hubert Green was so ugly when he was a baby, that his mother tied a pork chop around his neck to get the dog to play with him.
Larry Ziegler

The Super Models
I can't believe the actions of some of our top pros. They should have side jobs modelling for Pampers.
Fuzzy Zoeller

Dress For The Occasion
Trousers may now be worn by ladies on the course – but they must be removed before entering the clubhouse.
Notice in a golf club

Battle Of The Sexes
Dogs and Women Not Allowed.
Sign on golf club door

Hair-raising
Is that some kind of fashion accessory?
Fan, after a golf ball landed in an Irish maid's hair in New Jersey in the 1920s

Fair Play
All is fair in love and golf.
Anon

Pets Corner
Do not feed the alligators.
Sign outside the Marriot Hotel golf course in Orlando

Local Rule
If a reindeer eats your ball, drop a new one where the
incident occurred.
Rule at Bjorkliden Arctic Golfklubb in Sweden

Greenfingers
On the green, a ball lying in a hippo footmark may be lifted
and placed not nearer the hole without penalty.
Rule at Jinja GC in Uganda

Equality Of The Sexes
Ladies and gentlemen welcome regardless of sex.
Notice in a new golf club

Snakes Alive
If your ball lands within a club length of a rattlesnake, you
are allowed to move the ball.
Rule at club in Arizona

Mind Control
Playing Royal St George's is like trying to read the mind of a
beautiful woman. It can be difficult, but never onerous. It is
for reading, not bashing. You can be in the soup at St
George's, but it is delicious.
William Deedes

Dressed For The Occasion
Eric Sykes: 'What do you think of my tee shot?'
Isao Aoki: 'Very nice, but sleeves a little long!'

Birds Of A Feather
Suggest that all the birds living by the second green be given
diapers to protect the seat.
Comment in Royal St George's GC suggestion book [1952]

3. Star Quality

Case Closed
I've heard of golfers trying to get through the eye of a needle, but this takes some beating.
Fan, after Tony Jacklin's ball landed in a binocular case at the 1971 Open at Royal Birkdale

The Spoils Of Victory
Maybe I should go to a sports shop and buy a trophy. That's the only way I'm going to get one.
Severiano Ballesteros, in 1995 during a lean spell in his career

Exaggeration
The alligator thing was nothing big. I just saw a little five-foot alligator once near a water hole in Florida and flipped it over by its tail. That's easy. But the guy I was playing with made it sound like I wrestled it.
Andy Bean

Second Place
I did something by climbing over 113 golfers. The only thing is, there were 114 ahead of me.
Joanne Carner, after finishing second in the US Women's Open, after being 115th after the first round

Limits
I don't mind playing golf with Greg Norman, but I'll be damned if I'll go swimming with him.
Lee Trevino, on the golfer known as the 'Great White Shark'

Deep Throat
He couldn't swear as much as he would have liked to on the golf course.
Mrs Sean Connery, explaining the effects of a temporary loss of voice on her husband when he had laser surgery on his throat in 1992

Boiling Point
There's more tension in golf than in boxing because golfers bring it on themselves. It's silly really, because it's not as if the golf ball is going to jump up and belt you on the whiskers, is it?
Henry Cooper

Bing There

That was a great game of golf.
Last words of Bing Crosby

Spectator Sport

It was quite good fun watching John [Daly] dislodge a cubic yard of Kent every time he hit the ball. Even his divots were travelling further than my shots.
David Feherty

Crumbs Of Comfort

It is more satisfying to be a bad player at golf. The worse you play, the better you remember the occasional good shot.
Nubar Gulbenkian

What's In A Name?

Sounds like a fag winemaker from Modesto.
Jimmy Demaret on Gay Brewer

Danger

Gerry Ford [former American president] – the most dangerous driver since Ben Hur... It's not hard to find Gerry Ford on a golf course, you just follow the wounded...Gerry Ford has made golf a contact sport.
Bob Hope

Public Safety
I know I'm getting better at golf because I'm hitting
fewer spectators.
  Gerald Ford

Professional Solidarity
Every time you see him, he's got a face like a warthog that's
just been stung by a wasp.
  David Feherty, describing Scotland's Colin Montgomerie.
  When asked to confirm that remark, he said: 'What I said is that
  Colin looks like a bulldog licking pi*s off a nettle'

Self-induced Pleasure
I refuse to play golf with Errol Flynn. If I want to play with
a prick, I'll play with my own.
  W. C. Fields

Modest Ambition
I have no aspirations to be a millionaire. I just want to live
like one.
  'The Haig' – Walter Charles Hagen

Strength
His driving is unbelievable. I don't go that far on
my holidays.
  Ian Baker-Finch on John Daly

Bond's Law
The difference between a good golf shot and a bad one is the
same as the difference between a beautiful and a plain
woman – a matter of millimetres.
  Ian Fleming

Inaccurate
My golfing partner couldn't hit a tiled floor with a bellyful
of puke.
  David Feherty

Play Safe
If I'm on the course and lightning starts, I get inside fast. If
God wants to play through, let him.
  Bob Hope

Dedication
Pinky Kerr is on th' decline but refuses t'consult a doctor fer fear he'll tell him t'play golf.
Frank McKinney Hubbard

Loaded Deck
You'd better be careful any time you play golf with President Johnson – he always brings his own birdies.
Hubert H. Humphrey

Air Supply
Tee the ball high. Because years of experience have shown me that air offers less resistance to dirt.
Jack Nicklaus

Shooting From The Lip
Nick Faldo and Peter Oosterhuis were probably our top players around 1977 and the rest of us couldn't hit a cow's arse with a banjo.
Mark James, on the Ryder Cup team

Jungle Fever
He [Nick Faldo] has developed the best swing since Tarzan.
Colin M. Jarman

Around The World In 80-plus Strokes
Magellan went round the world in 1512 – which isn't too many strokes when you consider the distance.
Joe Laurie Jnr

Parental Obligations
I owe a lot to my parents – especially my mother and father.
Greg Norman

Framed
Most of the Europeans should be sponsored by zimmer frames – it's the same team as 10 years ago.
David Leadbetter, on the 1993 European Ryder Cup team

If You Can't Stand The Heat . . .
I play in the low 80s, if it's any hotter than that, I won't play.
Joe Lewis, comedian

Flexibility
Sometimes it stands for Stupid, sometimes it stands for Smart.
Hale S. Irwin, when asked what his middle initial stood for

The Royal Dane
Reporter: Would you like to play Hamlet?
Groucho Marx: Not unless he gives me a stroke a hole.

Earthquake
Arnold Palmer is going to be a great player. When he hits the ball, the earth shakes.
Gene Littler in 1954

Great Expectations
When Nicklaus plays well, he wins, when he plays badly, he comes second. When he's playing terribly, he's third.
Johnny Miller

Enthusiasm
He [Ballesteros] goes after a golf course the way a lion goes after a zebra.
Jim Murray

Frustration
I took up golf for the exercise and all I keep getting is holes-in-one.
Geoffrey Nunn, humourist

Safety Net
Oh well, no matter what happens, I can always dig ditches for a living.
Arnold Palmer

Jungle Book
I'm playing like Tarzan – and scoring like Jane.
Juan 'Chi Chi' Rodriguez

4. Sex, Lies and Videotape

An Undisputed Fact
And now to hole eight which is in fact, the eighth hole.
Peter Alliss

First Impressions
I saw a road runner and a coyote and I expected to see
Bugs Bunny.
*David Feherty, telling American journalists of his first
impressions of the USPGA Tour in 1994*

Three Into Two
It'll take three damn good shots to get up in two today.
Paul Dobson

Fidelity
That [not having a steady girlfriend in his bachelor days]
would be too much like playing on the same golf course all
the time!
Severiano Ballesteros

Womaniser
They say, 'Trevino is wondering whether to play a five- or
six-iron to the green', when all the time I'm gazing at some
broad in the third row of the gallery, wondering where my
wife is.
Lee Trevino

Whispering Blues
I don't like to watch golf on TV because I can't stand people
who whisper.
David Brenner

Fault
All golfers blame chance for other accidents, but accept full
responsibility when they hit a hole-in-one.
Alan Blakewell

Comparison
The difference between learning to play golf and learning to
drive a car is that in golf you never hit anything.
Jim Campbell

Review The Evidence
When ground rules permit a golfer to improve his lie, he can
either move his ball or change the story about his score.
Ian Edwards

Honesty
Nothing handicaps you so much in golf as honesty.
Oliver Cronin

The Truth And Nothing Less Than The Truth
In golf the ball usually lies poorly, but the player well.
William Davies

Creative Excuse
I have to fill eighteen cavities.
Dentist, explaining why he had to miss a boring party. He wanted to play a game of golf

When A Man Loves A Woman
I've avoided playing thirty-six holes in one day in a tournament for more than five years. The only time I would usually consider playing more than eighteen is when my wife Claudia insists that I give her a lesson.
Lee Trevino

Love On The Rocks?
Acquiring a new set of golf clubs is rather like getting married. The honeymoon is wonderful, but how things go after that depends on whether the courtship has properly tested the true compatibility of partners.
Peter Dobereiner

JUST MARRIED

So Sad When Good Love Goes Bad
I've lost 40 lbs since Christmas – make that 150 lbs, if you include my wife.
  David Feherty, on being separated from his wife

Job Description
A caddy is someone who accompanies the golfer and didn't see the ball either.
  Joe Francis

Confidence Building
Your bad days at golf are not at all serious to your fellow players. If anything, each of your bad shots builds the other fellow's ego.
  James Gallagher

Convivial Company
A golf cart is a method of transporting clubs that has one advantage – it can't count.
  Joachim Heinrich

Numeracy Skills
When you are playing golf, nothing counts like your opponent.
  Peter Holmes

The Book Of Evidence
Golf liars have one advantage over fishing liars; they don't have to show anything to prove it.
  Ian Howe

Japanese Whispers
The PGA tour has a simple test to see if a player is on drugs – if Isao Aoki speaks and the player understands him, the player is on something.
  Bob Hope

Slow Learner
Interviewee: I've always wanted to play golf, so I thought it would be a good thing to learn the rudiments of the game.
Interviewer: So have you learned much?
Interviewee: Yes, I have. How to hold a cue.

Marital Discord
That's what happens when you haven't been home in 18 years.
Lee Trevino, explaining why his wife divorced him

Biting Unfit
The shark with the bite of a fish finger.
Journalist, on Greg Norman

5. Business And Pleasure

Profit and Loss
I was the first golfer to make a million dollars – and to spend two.
Walter Hagen

Down On The Farm
If you can't break 85, you have no business on the golf
course. If you can break 85, you probably have no business.
Farmer's Almanac

Strike It Lucky
Yesterday, I was a poor Mexican. From now on, I'm going to
be a rich Spaniard.
Lee Trevino, after winning the 1968 US Open

A Game Resembling Golf
A sports encyclopedia says there are 300 kinds of games played
with balls. There are more than that played with golf balls alone.
Oliver Marsh

Shaky
I was swinging like a toilet door on a prawn trawler.
David Feherty

Suburbia
The average suburbanite either 'putters' around the house or
the golf course.
Frank Gallagher

State Of Mind
A well-adjusted man is one who can play golf as if it were
a game.
Harry Keane

Priorities
Fan: My golf clubs were stolen this morning.
Friend: That's terrible – where did you lose them?
Fan: In the car-park.
Friend: Did the thieves damage your car much?
Fan: I don't know – they stole that too!

Options
I may buy the Alamo and give it back to Mexico.
  Lee Trevino, on his $30,000 prize-money after winning the Masters

Rejection
I'm not going to buy this place, it doesn't have any inside plumbing.
  Trevino, after seeing the Alamo

Resilience
The real test of golf – and life – is not keeping out of the rough, but getting out after we are in.
  Henry Lash

Senility
Old golfers never die – they simply lose their drive.
  Paul Nixon

With A Little Help From My Friends
Few people carry a heavier burden farther than a golf caddy.
  Stephen Nolan

Self-criticism
That was a Shi'ite effort.
  David Feherty, describing a bad putt in the Dubai Desert Classic

Incentive
I have to win this tournament. My wife bought $50,000 worth of furniture last week. And you should see the house she built around it.
  Lee Trevino

Silence Is Golden
The hardest thing to learn about golf is keeping quiet about it.
  George Houghton

Energy Saver
If you're going to throw a club in temper, it's important to throw it ahead of you, in the direction of the green. That way, you don't waste energy going back to pick it up.
Tommy Bolt

Laughing Matter
Funny game golf, especially the way I play it.
Henry Cooper

Mind Over Matter
Golf is a game that is played on a five-inch course – the distance between the ears.
Bobby Jones

Analogy
A golf shot entails merely hitting a half-volley straight back to the bowler without giving a catch.
Henry Longhurst

Loquacious
It seems that the most reticent of men on other subjects no sooner takes to golf than eloquence descends on him.
John Hogben

Objective
If the golfer's object was merely to sink the ball in the hole, he could walk around the course with a bag of golf balls and drop each one in.
Arnold Lunn

Pressure Zone
You don't know what pressure is in golf until you play for five bucks with only two in your pocket.
Lee Trevino

'Simple' Instructions
When you come to play golf ye maun hae a heid!
Charles MacDonald

Temperance
If you drink, don't drive. Don't even putt.
Dean Martin

Disqualifier
If I had my way, any man guilty of golf would be ineligible for any office of trust in the United States.
Henry L. Mencken

Potential
Unless his putting stroke deserts him, Seve should become the richest Spaniard since Queen Isabella.
Jim Murray

Redeeming Qualities
I have a bad swing, a bad stance and a bad grip, but my bank manager loves me.
Lee Trevino

Falsehood
Income tax has made more liars out of the American people than golf.
Will Rogers

Dysfunctional Family
The place of the father in the modern suburban family is a very small one, particularly if he plays golf, which he usually does.
Bertrand Russell

Bite The Hand That Feeds
I wish it had bitten me a little lower down.
David Feherty, after he was bitten by an adder at Wentworth and his arm swelled to twice its normal size

Big Bucks
I'm going to win so much money this year that my caddy will make the top twenty money-winners list.
Lee Trevino

10

Horse Racing Hoots

The humour, intelligence and verbal cock-ups of jockeys, owners, punters, bookies and true blue royalty are all reflected in this compendium of racing snippets – over a century of racing as it is spoken. Heady thrills in the saddle, flawed aspirations to greatness, the bang of the stable door, the clink of the hoof on concrete and wonderful heroes as well as villains and victims are part of the daily currency of racing. If you are seeking a chuckle, it is an odds-on bet you will unearth it here.

1. Sound and vision

Talking Through the Rear End
Racing results farting...starting at...and I'm not even sure
what that is actually... It looks like Newcastle.
   Tony Adamson, from Sporting Gaffes

Wired For Sound?
Did you see me on the radio?
   *Delighted jockey Tony Dobbin, to his changing-room valet after
his first Cheltenham win*

Apt Title
Pat on the Back
   Title of Pat Eddery's autobiography

The Dream Ticket
The simple truth is that some of our racecourses are poorly
run and unimaginatively managed and couldn't attract extra
customers if Arkle, Desert Orchid, Nijinsky and the
Archangel Gabriel all appeared on the same card.
   Sporting Life

Media Management
He is a man of exquisite courtesy and addresses even the
humbler members of the racing press as 'sir'.
   Comment about Jack Colling

Miss Your Sights
It's not going to be the same, not seeing his bottom going
around in the air.
   Jimmy Lindley, on Lester Piggot's 'final' retirement in 1995

All In The Game
The Game Spirit Chase, named after Game Spirit, a lovely
horse owned by Her Majesty the Queen Mother, who
dropped dead here after a long and distinguished career.
   Peter Bromley from Sporting Gaffes

A Fine Figure
He seemed rather well endowed.
   Anonymous woman racegoer on a streaker at the 1994 Derby

Green Fingers
I remember somebody asked me how I was going to celebrate after I won my first Derby. I told them I was going home to cut the grass.
Lester Piggott

It's The Real Thing
Sorry, I've had too much Coke, I'm way up...
Clare Balding, on BBC radio. She later explained: 'I meant, I drank too much Coke in the car on the way'

Word Perfect
The unpronounceable Irkutsk is 14/1.
Commentator on SIS, after pronouncing the unpronounceable

'And There's A Faller'
It [the Grand National] was a tremendous race, with four finishers out of 30 starters, so by the end there were far more BBC commentators than horses.
Clive James

Literal Truth
When those stalls open, the horses are literally going to explode.
Brough Scott

Sartorial Inelegance
Looking like a hedge dragged through a man backwards.
Sunday Express *description of John McCririck*

Acid Drops 1
A sexist paddock pillock with all the charm of an armpit.
The Daily Star, *on John McCririck*

Acid Drops 2
He reckons he's a sexual athlete. But the bejewelled, arm-waving John McCririck looks more like a beached whale than a good bet between the sheets.
Carole Malone, in the Daily Star

Role Reversal
Peter O'Sullevan is the race of voicing.
Richard Pitman

The Unforgiven
It is unforgivable to deny racegoers facilities for losing their money swiftly and painlessly.
Hugh McIlvanney

Beauty and the Beast
The bizarre thought of Willie Carson looking like Britt Ekland came from two separate quarters this week.
Alan Fraser, commenting on entries for a look-alike competition

Puzzling Logic
They've got well under just over two circuits to go.
SIS commentary at Ayr

Racing Certainty?
. . . and there's the unmistakable figure of Joe Mercer . . . or is it Lester Piggott?
Brough Scott

Get To The Bottom Of It
Their bottoms are the wrong shape.
Lester Piggott, on female jockeys

Sweet Memories
The Sussex course resembled a sticky toffee pudding.
   Geoff Lester

Coincidence?
We have before had occasion to compliment the sagacity and intelligence displayed by Mr Cartwright's horses. They never win when they are favourites, but always when long odds are to be obtained about them. The public ought to be grateful to them.
   Sporting Life, *1865*

New Identity
The cynics call it the Bleeders' Cup.
   Tim Richards

Painful Dilemma
Given the choice between a vasectomy without an anaesthetic, and listening to Lord Oaksey ramble on about past Whitbread Gold Cups on the Morning Line, I would make the former a shade of odds-on.
   Mark Winstanley

Sexual Stimulation
There are two things in life guaranteed to get me excited. The first is Anna Lee tackled up in stockings, the second is the start of the Flat at Doncaster.
   Mark Winstanley

Lucky Charm
I usually wear my underwear inside-out for good luck.
   Laffit Pincay

Injury
I've had worse falls tumbling out of bed.
   Lester Piggott after his horrific fall in the Breeders Cup in 1992

For God's Sake
Secretariat [Horse of the Year in 1972 and '73] and Rivia Ridge are the most famous pair of stablemates since Joseph and Mary.
   Dick Schaap

2. Jockeys

Money, Money, Money
I'd rather have a cheque.
Lester Piggott, when offered 'a most attractive Brazilian stone set of ashtrays' by grateful owner Robert Ellis

Survival
There are two important rules in horse-riding. The first is to mount the horse. The second is to stay mounted.
Edward Andrews

Job Description
Riding is the art of keeping a horse between yourself and the ground.
Alan Adams

Inconsiderate
You've got no chance with a race like the Derby – the bastards are all trying.
Anon head lad

Behind The Public Image
They say that Lester [Piggott] is mean, but that isn't true – he's twice as mean as they say. They say that he's difficult to get along with, and that's not true either – he's impossible.
Anon

Priorities
How did the runners at Taunton perform?
Heart attack victim Chester Barnes' first question after recovery

All Ends Up
People ask me why I ride with my bottom in the air. Well, I've got to put it somewhere.
Lester Piggott

The Young Ones
Horses and jockeys mature earlier than people – which is why horses are admitted to race tracks at the age of two, and jockeys before they are old enough to shave.
Dick Beddoes

All or Nothing
Kenneth [Oliver] has only two gears – fast asleep or flat out.
Harry Beeby

Bum Deal
The St Mark's Square Bum Pincher.
Nickname for Frankie Dettori

Back to Basics
It's still the same. One leg each side.
Lester Piggott, when asked if it would be difficult to readjust to riding on his comeback

Hedging His Bets
Can't really say, but whatever beats me will win it.
John Francome, replying when asked who would win his two-runner exhibition with Lester Piggott

The Galloping Granny
I've seen that description 'The Galloping Granny' in countless newspaper headlines and it's not true. I've no children.
Rosemary Henderson, who finished 5th in the 1994 Grand National on Fiddler's Pike

Perspective
I obviously feel let down to some extent.
Michael Hills, after he was sacked by his father – trainer Barry

Aimless
He jumped on his horse and galloped off madly in all generations.
Stephen Leacock, on an amateur jockey with a very short career – one race

Public Persona
He [Lester Piggott] has a face like a well-kept grave.
Jack Leach

Small Is Beautiful
I was too small to be a window-cleaner and too big to be a garden gnome.
Adrian Maguire, on why he became a jockey

It's A Bummer
I can honestly say it's a pain in the arse.
> *Injured jockey Richard Fox, on the pin in his damaged leg which had drifted out of position*

Crib-tic
I'm riding out for every stable bar Bethlehem at the moment.
> *Dean McKeown*

Seating Arrangements
Girls who ride horses don't necessarily have big behinds.
> *Ann Moore*

No Holding
Never catch a loose horse. You could end up all day holding the f*****g thing.
> *Lester Piggott*

The Domino Effect
If a horse runs badly, the trainer kicks the jockey, the jockey kicks the horse, they all kick the stable cat and then there's nobody left to kick except the handicapper.
> *Christopher Mordaunt*

Self-protection
The real charm of having Lester ride for you is that it gets him off the other fellow's horse.
Vincent O'Brien

Foolish Behaviour
There are, they say, fools, bloody fools, and men who remount in a steeplechase.
John Oaksey

The Knick Of Time
It was just as well I was wearing knickers. Some of the ladies don't.
Helen Pewter, whose breeches split completely as she fell from her horse

Leave Well Enough Alone
Jeremy Lee [trainer]: I've got to speak to my old school, Lester, and tell them all I know about racing. What should I tell them?
Lester Piggott: Tell 'em you've got the flu!

Polite Conversation
Would you like to speak to the horse?
Mark Pitman, answering queries on his mobile phone about one of his horses

Wise Move

Decided not to get married in 1981.

Billy Norris, when asked the highlight of his career

Honesty Is The Best Policy

Lincoln went down in history as 'Honest Abe', but he never was a jockey. If he had been a jockey, he might have gone down as just 'Abe'.

Will Rogers

Dual Ambitions

I always dreamt of being a millionaire and a racing driver.

Lester Piggott. (He earned the money and got 10 speeding tickets in the same period)

Prophetic

What did I Tulyar?

Charlie Smirke, after winning the Derby on Tulyar in 1952

True Confessions?

There's three things I can confess to. Since I was 21 I have been drunk almost every night; I never sold a race, which is more than some can say; and I never kissed a lass against her will.

Nineteen times Classic winner Bill Scott, on his deathbed in 1848. In relation to the final two confessions, it is probable he was suffering from selective memory!

Comparisons

She's like Linford Christie – without the lunch-box.

Frankie Dettori, on Lochsong

Loose Running

A loose horse is any horse sensible enough to get rid of its rider at an early stage and carry on unencumbered.

Clive James

3. Owners

Ethics and Politics

Over here [France], racing is considered immoral. When an MP becomes a Minister, he sells his racehorse.

Janet Slade

Below The Belt
In racing, to insult a man's horse is worse than insulting his wife.
John Oaksey

Telltale Signs
If in the paddock the owner is surrounded by a herd of young children, don't back his horse. But if the owner is accompanied by a beautiful lady, plunge to the hilt.
Robert Morley

The Perfect Match
I'd like to find a man as good as him for a husband.
Peggy Augustus, owner of Husband, winner of Canada's Rothmans International in 1993

Beguiling
The majority of yearlings are regrettably the product of matings designed for the catwalk rather than the race track.
Patrick Brain

Silly Distraction
How amusing racing would be if it were not for the horses. They take people's minds off conversation.
Viscount Castelrosse

Confusion
My horse was in the lead, coming down the home stretch, but the caddy fell off.
Samuel Goldwyn

Pitfalls and Pratfalls
Racing is like politics – it's full of good rogues.
Eddie Harty

Sales Pitch
I didn't know I had such a valuable horse until I heard the auctioneer describe him.
Robert Morley

My Lips Are Sealed
I'm too superstitious to talk about them [superstitions].
William I. Mott

Grief
It's been a tough year for me, owning such a superb filly but losing my wife.
Racehorse owner

4. The Gambling Bug

Lottery
A racehorse is the only horse which can take thousands of people for a ride at the same time.
Anon

Mug's Game
In most betting shops you will see three windows marked 'Bet Here', but only one window with the legend 'Pay Out'.
Jeffrey Bernard

Access All Areas
I reckon I am an ordinary sort of chap and I must certainly be approachable because punters are always approaching me after a horse of ours runs badly!
Jack Berry

Prayer Power
I know it's difficult for you Lord, we have so many runners.
Father Sean Breen, saying Mass for Irish runners at the Cheltenham Festival

Consumer Advice
The only tip I can give on jumpers is – where to buy them in London.
Flat trainer Henry Cecil

All or Nothing
Remember – Lady Godiva put all she had on a horse.
W. C. Fields

Addiction
Racing is just like damn drinking: momentary excitement and wretched intervals; full consciousness of the mischievous effects of the habit and equal difficulty in abstaining from it.
Charles Greenville

Tragic Accident
I met with an accident on the way to the track;
I arrived safely.
   Joe E. Lewis

Hope Springs Eternal
In betting on races, there are two elements that are never lacking
– hope as hope, and an incomplete recollection of the past.
   Edward V. Lucas

A Dog's Life
Anybody who finds it easy to make money on the horses is
probably in the dog food business.
   Franklin P. Jones

Right and Wrong
I backed the right horse, but the wrong horse went and won.
   H. A. Jones & H. Herman

Poet's Corner
I have seen flowers come out in stony places,
and kind things done by men with ugly faces,
And the Gold Cup won by the worst horse at the races.
   John Masefield

Legal Tender
A bookie is just a pickpocket who lets you use your own hands.
   Henry Morgan

Fatal Attraction
Racing is like fishing; it's the one that gets away that
fascinates and intrigues.
   Robert Morley

Within The Law
Racing is the best fun you can have with your clothes on.
   Andy Orkney

The Price Is Right
You can have 50/1 Glory, Boredom at 7/4 or Money at 1/2.
   *Bookie, on Lester Piggott's reason for returning to the saddle
   in 1991*

Right Time. Wrong Place.
Racegoer: Thank God I've got here. I'm not too late for the National, am I?

He wasn't. The only problem was that he went to Haydock Park instead of Aintree!

On The Glory Trail
The only man who makes money following the races is one who does it with a broom and a shovel.

Elbert Hubbard

Funny Money
They're not really bookies these days, they're just debt collectors.

Jack Ramsden

Principled Opposition
Much as bookmakers are opposed to law-breaking, they are not bigoted about it.

Damon Runyon

A Mug's Game
A mug is born every minute of the day, and thank Gawd, some of them live.

Bookie, Fred Swindell

Odds-on
I am not one of the people who believe that the main reason why a chap becomes a bookmaker is because he is too scared to steal and too heavy to become a jockey.

Noel Whitcome

Paternity Dispute
It is frequently asserted in bookmaking circles that my mother and father met only once, and then for a very brief period.

Lord Wigg

The 3 F's
There are three racecourses beginning with the letter F – namely Fontwell, Folkestone and effing Plumpton.

Fred Winter attributed

5. Officialdom

Scandal
It is scandalous that they allow horses in here [Ascot]!
Anon actress

Dress Sense
Ladies in hot pants will only be allowed to enter the Royal Enclosure at Ascot if the general effect is satisfactory.
Ascot authorities' decree in 1971

Living Dolls
The Jockey Club have issued a writ against the Texan who introduced Cabbage Patch dolls. They claim that they have been making them for years – and calling them stewards.
John Francome

Helpful Suggestion
The form book should be written in braille for the benefit of the stewards.
Clive Graham

Incompetence
He couldn't start a race for white mice.
David Nicholson, on new Aintree starter Simon Morant

THE CHEESE CUP

The Origin Of The Species
Stewards are, on the whole, simple folk. Most of them come from a social class in which inbreeding has taken its toll.
Paul Haigh

Parallel Lines
Desert Orchid and I have a lot in common. We are both greys; vast sums of money are riding on our performance; the Opposition hopes we will fall at the first fence; and we are both carrying too much weight.
Norman Lamont

Short-sighted
Officialdom's refusal to pee into a bottle is as myopic as Mr Magoo.
Andy Orkney

Panties
Knicker elastic.
Jenny Pitman's dismissive description of the starting tape in the Grand National that never was

Imperial
We want a man, like Caesar's wife, above suspicion, of independent means, a perfect knowledge of the form and actual conditions of every public horse, without having the slightest interest in any stable.
Admiral Rous' CV of a public handicapper in 1855. He then decided he was the only one suitable for the job!

6. Trainers

A Helpful Hint
It was a very good training feat by trainer Ronnie O'Leary to park the knacker's van outside the horse's box.
Steve Hammond, whose horse Concert Paper won after three years of failures

The Surgeon's Knife
He's had more operations than Joan Collins – and maybe more men working on him.
Jenny Pitman, on Gold Cup winner Burrough Hill Lad

Failure

My biggest failure as a trainer – I never made a gentleman of
Lester Piggott.

Jack Jarvis

And The Last Shall Be First

You know, that's the best race he's ever run.

Trainer John Jenkins, on one of his horses that finished last

In His Master's Footsteps

I'm now only 43 Classic winners behind Vincent.

*Michael Kauntze, ex-assistant to Vincent O'Brien, after his
Kooyonga won the Irish 1000 Guineas in 1991*

Amnesia?

That's the way I remember it.

*'Bald Eagle' Whittingham, explaining why he listed his hair
colour as brown when applying for his licence*

Chronology

Lester is the greatest jockey of the century, of all time – even
of the decade.

Robert Sangster, on Lester Piggott

Burdensome

He was a bit disappointing last year when he was very top-
heavy and had a wind problem.

Peter Savill

Good Friday

If Jesus Christ rode his flaming donkey like you just rode that
horse, then he deserved to be crucified.

The late trainer Fred Rimell, to Jim Old

Well-balanced diet

Yes, but I can't eat a whole one.

Trainer Rod Simpson, when asked if he liked Wales

Gentle Touch

I have spent more time feeling Delius's front legs than my
wife Carol's!

Richard Lee

Miracle Cure
If I'd been running around all my life with an inflamed testicle
and it was suddenly sorted out, I'm sure I'd run faster.
  Michael Kauntze, explaining Selkirk's *improved form in
  winning the Queen Elizabeth Stakes after an operation to
  remove his testicle*

No Way
I don't have any [superstitions]. They're bad luck.
  Jose Adeon Santos

Consideration
I hope he has not hurt his foot.
  *'Bald Eagle' Whittingham, after getting a nasty gash on his
  head when his champion horse Sunday Silence kicked him*

7. Equine Matters

Putting The Cart Before The Horse
Raymond Brooks-Ward: And now I'm joined by the winner.
Otto, congratulations on a great win for Germany.
Interviewee: I'm sorry, my name is Steven. Otto is the name of
my horse!

Oh No, It's Not!
It's John Reid.
  Emlyn Hughes' identification on A Question of Sport *of a
  mud-splattered jockey. In fact, it was Princess Anne!*

Public Performance
Polo players do it in public – without scaring the horses.
  Colin M. Jarman

Health Warning
If brains were a virus, jockeys would be the healthiest people
in the country.
  Philip Mitchell

Inside Knowledge
The American horses know the fences like the back of
their hand.
  Harvey Smith

Stable Environment
Go anywhere in England where there are natural, wholesome, contented and really nice English people; and what do you always find? That the stables are the real centre of the house.

George Bernard Shaw

The Road Not Taken
I should like to be a horse.

Elizabeth Windsor attributed

Local Heroes
Donkey races open to the residents of the Parish.

Sign seen at a country race meeting

Upstairs, Downstairs
There are two classes in good society in England: the equestrian classes and the neurotic classes.

George Bernard Shaw

11
Ruck and Roll

A part from their unceasing curiosity as 'words of wisdom', sporting quotations enable us to peer through the looking glass darkly, as it were, and glimpse the attitudes and philosophies of its practitioners. Sport's verbal legacy invariably reflects a high sophistication, mature wisdom and a cultivated social sense and serves as an invaluable sociological barometer and cultural index. If this sounds very serious, it is because it is a blatant effort to give some spurious status to the following light-hearted romp through decades of rugby tomfoolery. In this collection rugby's high and mighty do not escape the barb, but there is much humour. This fascinating, sometimes cynical, always witty compilation will delight all those addicted to the sport played by women and men with odd shaped balls!

1. What's the name of the game?

Definition

Rugby is a game played by men with odd-shaped balls.
  Anon

Pre-emptive Strike

Modern rugby players like to get their retaliation in first.
  Kim Fletcher

Productivity

A forward's usefulness to his side varies as to the square of
his distance from the ball.
  Clarrie Gibbons, sportswriter

Out Of Bounds

That one was a bit inebriated, just like one of my golf shots.
  Bill McLaren, describing a penalty kick

Afters

Don't look, boys. Concentrate on the game. There'll be plenty
of time for that later.
  *Scottish captain Jim Aitken, during the half-time team talk at
  Twickenham in 1993, when two buxom streakers graced the pitch*

I Don't Like Mondays
The main difference between League and Union is that now I get my hangovers on Monday instead of Sunday.
Tom David

Alphabet City
Signals ambiguity should be avoided. A word sign beginning with the letter 'P' was the signal for the forwards to go right. When, predictably, Gareth Edwards called 'psychology', half the forwards went left.
Carwyn James

A Female Perspective
The women sit, getting colder and colder, on a seat getting harder and harder, watching oafs getting muddier and muddier.
Virginia Graham, on a rugby match

Mistaken Messages
Rugby captain: Nineteen sixty two [a coded signal before a throw-in from the lineout.]
Supporter: Jesus, they're ordering the champagne already!

Parting Shot
I have done for rugby what Quasimodo did for coat-hangers.
Tom McNab, the former England rugby coach

Small Change
You ask me if headquarters worry about change. Well, hardly – everything is paid for by cheque.
RFU official, on BBC Radio Sport

Touché
The way you are taught to make contact in rugby is with your shoulder, leaning forward. This means that the most vulnerable part is protected. And anyway, I'd argue that men are much more vulnerable to . . . underhand tactics, shall we say.
English ladies' rugby captain Emma Mitchell in answer to the question: 'Wouldn't women rugby players be vulnerable to breast damage?'

2. The International Dimension

The French Connection
I wouldn't play the French at marbles, never mind Rugby League. All we will ever learn off them is how to fight and spit and bite each other.
Alex Murphy

Colour
New Zealand rugby is a colourful game – you get all black and blue.
Anon

Upwardly Mobile
Q: What's new about the big Irish Softie?
A: He's getting paid for playing rugby.
Graffiti on Dublin wall

Physical Contact
There were at least five instances of people being grabbed by the testicles. Neath is the bag-snatching capital of Wales.
Australian rugby coach Bob Dwyer, after his side's victory over Neath

Identity Crisis
Naas Botha was one of the most prodigious goal-kickers of all time but attracted a lot of controversy in South Africa because of his apparent reluctance to pass the ball. After he kicked his club side's 24 points to give them victory in the Cup Final, he found himself sitting beside another man on the plane. Botha was a bit surprised that his companion said nothing to him. After half an hour of total silence, he turned around and said: 'I don't think you realise who I am, I'm probably the most famous rugby player in South Africa.'
His companion responded quietly: 'I don't think you realise who *I* am. I play for your team. I'm your first centre!'

It's Not Who You Are, But Where You Are
The state of British sport is mostly serious, but never hopeless. The state of Irish sport is usually hopeless, but never serious.
Noel Henderson

Puzzle
What the Ireland-England game at Lansdowne Road proved was that the England pack was not only over the hill, it was over the Himalayas.

Sean Diffley, struggling to comprehend the selection of 16 Englishmen, and just two Irish, for the British Lions tour in the immediate aftermath of Ireland's 17-3 victory over England in 1993

The Gladiators
When you play Munster in Thomond Park, you can appreciate how the early Christians felt in the Coliseum.

Earl Kirton, former All Black

Media Verdict
In New Zealand, if the Prime Minister died, and if he had played for the All Blacks, the headline in the papers would be: 'All Black dies.'

David Thomas

I Was Only Trying To Be Helpful
Woman in her birthday suit: 'Darling, I love you.'
Her lover: 'Your face is so beautiful that I will have it painted in gold. Your breasts are so magnificent that I will have them painted in silver. Your legs are so shapely that I will have them painted in platinum.'
Two Welsh rugby players looking in through the keyhole: 'We're two painters from Pontypool!'

The Big Softie
Don't ask me about emotion in a Welsh dressing-room. I cry when I watch *Little House on the Prairie*.

Bob Norster

Balance
The Irish treat you like royalty before and after a game, and kick you to pieces during it.

Jeff Probyn

Positive Thinking
There's only one man allowed to say: 'There's nothing wrong with defeat,' and that's Nelson Mandela's chiropodist.

Jack Rowell

Funny Tummy

Listen, pal. Where I come from, you eat everything that's put down in front of you.

Scottish prop Gerry McGuinness, following his release from hospital, explaining why he had eaten lotus-leaf garnish during a tour of Japan

Animal, Vegetable or Melbourner?

Anyone who doesn't watch Rugby League is not a real person. He's a cow's hoof, an ethnic, senile or comes from Melbourne.

John Singleton

Tactical Ineptitude

Wales didn't even have enough imagination to thump someone in the line-out when the ref wasn't looking.

J.P.R. Williams

3. Players

Tough Cookie

If you broke (Gareth) Chilcott's arm, he'd kick you. If you broke his leg, he'd bite you. And if you took all his teeth out, he would headbutt you.

Nick Farr-Jones

All or Nothing

There is no such thing as 'a lack of confidence'. You either have it or you don't.

Rob Andrew

Mistaken Identity

English official at a post-match dinner: 'The soup was tepid.'
Scottish lock Alister Campbell: 'I thought it was chicken!'

Bull's Eye

Carling himself epitomises England's lack of skills – he has speed and bulk, but plays like a castrated bull.

David Campese

Fitness

Training takes the edge off my game.

Willie Duggan

Keeping Up With The Competition

'I'm stamping that bloody snail which has been following me around since the match started!'

A totally unfit Willie Duggan, playing in a summer friendly, asked why he was stamping on the ground

Retirement

Old rugby players never die – they simply have their balls taken away.

Anon

Streaker

Bill [Beaumont], there's a guy just run on the park with your backside on his chest.

Steve Smith, as a topless woman, Erica Roe, raced across the pitch when England played Australia in 1982

Split Down The Middle

Every time I went to tackle him, Horrocks went one way, Taylor the other, and all I got was the bloody hyphen.

Mick English, on Phil Horrocks-Taylor

A Class Act

I said to the manager, 'This is supposed to be a five-star hotel and there's a bloody hole in the roof.' He turned around and said, 'That's where you can see the five stars from.'

Gordon Brown

Loneliness
The only thing you're ever likely to get at the end of an English backline is chilblains.
David Campese

Divine Qualities
Did you say *in* the water or *on* the water?
Aussie journalist questions the management statement that David Campese was jogging in water in order to ease a groin strain

The Late, Late Show
At Bath we won many a game in the last minute. We had so many great escapes, I half-expected to look across to the replacement bench and see Steve McQueen.
Ben Clarke

No Flattery
As bald as a coot [Brian Bevan]. No teeth in his head. A skeleton in braces.
Arthur Clues

Mistaken Identity
Let's get right behind Wayne Gooley here.
England captain Paul Dodge, introducing debutant Wade Dooley to the English team

Positive Advantage
Sure, if it was not for the fags, I would be offside all day long.
Willie Duggan, when asked once in a radio interview if his smoking was a major problem for him fitness-wise. [Duggan was one of a rare group of players who always made a point of bringing a pack of cigarettes with him onto the training field]

Time Talking
I like to get in one really good tackle early in the game, even if it is late.
Ray Gravell

Job Search
I discovered that I had no talent nor vocation for any job – so I joined the Civil Service!
Moss Keane

Money Troubles

When I heard that the Rugby Union were on the line, I thought it might be a query about my expenses!

Damian Hopley, following his late call-up to the English squad in 1991

Sacred Writing

The Holy Writ of Gloucester Rugby Club demands: first, that the forwards shall win the ball, second that the forwards shall keep the ball, and third, the backs shall buy the beer.

Doug Ibbotson

High Energy

Brian Bevan could jink like a crazed pin-ball and hare like a barmy rabbit.

Frank Keating

Bob's Your Uncle

He [Bob Hiller] had the hair of a city slicker, and the hoofing toecap of a Tunisian mule.

Frank Keating

Regional Side

We've lost seven of our last eight matches. Only team that we have beaten was Western Samoa. Good job we didn't play the whole of Samoa.

Gareth Davies

Rough Stuff

Barrister during a court case: Do you know any Barbarians? [local gang of motorbikers]
Witness: Yes, John Jeffrey!

Tender Hands

It's a lot better. I've been to see a chiropodist.

A Kelso forward, when asked how his bad back was. In fact, he had consulted a chiropractor!

Bop Until You Drop

Geoff Cooke said that when he was finished with me, I'd be fit to drop. I was, and he did.

Dewi Morris

Bad Chocolate

I've seen better centres in a box of Black Magic.
  Joe McPartlin

Fast Slow

That's the first time I've seen a try scored live and in slow-motion at the same time.
  Jim Renwick, on a try for Bruce Hay – who was not known for his speed

The Voice

Eddie Waring has done as much for our sport as Cyril Smith would do for hang-gliding.
  Reg Bowden

Get Smart

Colin [Smart] may not have looked too good, but he smelled lovely.
  Steve Smith, commenting on Smart's aftershave

Creative Adaptation

It's an oop-an-under.
  Eddie Waring

Put Down

He [Gareth Chilcott] is green around the gills and a stranger to the lavatory.
  Jack Rowell

Eggs-actly 1

Bobby Windsor: 'I want one egg boiled for exactly 26 seconds and I want another one boiled for 25 minutes 14 seconds. And I want three slices of toast which are pale gold on one side and burned pure black on the other.'
Waiter: 'But, sir. That's simply not possible. We can't go to all the trouble to fulfill an order like that.'
Windsor: 'Oh yes you can, sonny boy. That's exactly what you dished up to me yesterday!'

Eggs-actly 2

Waiter: What kind of omelette would you like?
Bobby Windsor: One with eggs in it.

4. Rough Stuff

At The Frontiers
The front row is an immensely technical place where brain
and brawn collide; it is one which has fascinated me since I
played with a prop whose shorts caught fire during a game
as a consequence of carrying a light for his half-time fag.
Bill Lothian

Tactical Awareness
We had decided to go out in the first half to soften them up
and kick the proverbial sh*t out of them. And it went so well
for us, that we had a quick word at half-time and decided to
kick the sh*t out of them in the second half!
Willie Duggan

IQ
Playing in the second row doesn't require a lot of intelligence
really. You have to be bloody crazy to play there for a start.
Bill Beaumont

Mourning
Forward play is like a funeral. You have to get in front, with
the family; not behind with the friends.
Michael Benazet

Motivation

We were so fired up, when the referee ran on to the pitch, three of us tackled him.

Graham Dawe

Blood Sport

The only doubt in my mind was whether rugby isn't too dangerous a game – for the spectators.

Robert Lynd

Period Of Adjustment

Like a woman, different scrummaging machines can take some getting used to.

Ian McGeechan

Misconceptions

It seems a neat game, but do they really bite ears off?

Elizabeth Taylor

The Tooth Fairy's Legacy

I think Brian's gnashers are the kind you get from a DIY shop and hammer in yourself. He is the only player we have who looks like a French forward.

Paul Rendall, on his team-mate Brian Moore

Controlled Aggression

Man is a fighting animal and rugby is a civilised (almost always, anyway) blood sport.

Wilfrid Wooller

Perseverance

In my time I've had my knee put out, broken my collar-bone, had my nose smashed, a rib broken, lost a few teeth, and smashed my ankle, but as soon as I get a bit of bad luck I'm going to quit the game.

J. W. Robinson

12

Snooker from the Lip

Despite the outward calm of snooker players, as we shall discover, there is plenty of invective in the sport. Whoever said: 'Don't get mad [or was it *angry*?] – get even' must have been a snooker player! In their turbulent love affair with the game of many colours, fans of this obsession will rejoice in these true confessions, Freudian slip-ups, naked affronts and of course those victims of foot-in-mouth disease – the great and the good, the bad and the ugly. These on-the-record and off-the-cuff remarks offer an engaging insight into the wicked humour and polished impromptu of the world of snooker.

1. Personalities

When Two Is One
A two-frame lead is really only one.
Eddie Charlton

Oversight
Fred Davis: Where's the table?
Tournament organiser: We thought you'd bring it with you.

Pillow Talk
I think it's a great idea to talk during sex, as long as it's about snooker.
Steve Davis

The Glory Game
Less than perfect financial circumstances are the keenest spur to further endeavour.
Joe Davis, otherwise known as 'The Emperor of Pot', 'The Wizard of Pot', 'The King of the Cue', 'the Mercurial Maestro of the Baize', 'The Sultan of Snooker' and 'Potato Face'

Bare Message
Poll tax my bum.
Slogan on balloon worn by Christian Hennessey, snooker's first streaker

The Bobbit Factor
When I beat a man at pool, he seems to think he's had his willy chopped off.
Sue Thompson

If Only
I would have won if he hadn't turned up.
Cliff Wilson, after losing to Steve Davis

Behind Every Great Player . . .
Take everything I've got, including the wife, but leave my cue behind.
Ray Reardon, known variously as 'The Prince of Darkness', 'Dracula', 'Young Banger', 'The Welsh Corgi' and 'The Chief Inspector'

Legend
I know I've got a reputation like George Best, I've found that it helps being World Champion, especially at snooker. I always tell them [women] I'm a great potter. They know what I mean.
Alex Higgins

No Contest
If I had to choose between sex and snooker, I'd choose snooker.
Steve Davis

So Clever
Frame and Fortune
Title of Steve Davis' autobiography

Fitness Test
I like my players to be fit, but it's hard with someone like Jimmy White who trains on vodka and nightclubs.
Barry Hearn

Safety Net
Mr Higgins is not seriously hurt. He landed on his head.
A policeman, giving the good news after Alex left his girlfriend's flat through a first-floor window

Snooker from the Lip

Return To Form
I haven't played as well as that since London Bridge was a lighthouse.
Pat Houlihan

Intact
I'm disappointed, but not dissipated.
Alex Higgins, after losing to Willie Thorne

Simply Red
I've cleared the reds. Where are the bloody colours?
Melbourne Inman, knocking down a row of red lamps while driving off in his car

Seeing Red
That miss on the red will go straight out of my head as soon as I collect my pension book.
John Parrott

Speedie
I'm not quick enough to challenge Desert Orchid, but I'm quicker around the bend.
Alex Higgins

Top Billing
I wanted to be billed as Alexander the Great. Anyway, he wasn't as fast as me. Now I'm Hurricane Higgins.
Alex Higgins

Windy
My mates call me 'The Wind', actually.
Jimmy White, on his nickname 'The Whirlwind'

Jim'll Fix It
Jimmy White has the nervous system of a fighter pilot on amphetamines.
Clive James

Calamity
I went to the optician and received the most disappointing piece of good news I have ever had. My eyes were OK.
Cliff Thorburn

Brevity Is The Soul Of Wit
I'm monosyllabic, if that's the word.
Steve Davis

Explosive
'Hurricane' Higgins did for snooker what Guy Fawkes did
for fireworks.
Colin M. Jarman

2. Chess with Balls

Footloose
The British Board of Censors will not pass any seduction
scene unless the seducer has one foot on the floor. Apparently
sex in England is something like snooker.
Fred Allen

Tip-off
It had more tips than a head waiter.
Dennis Taylor, on an unreliable cue

Losing The Head
The most unkindest cut of all.
*J. C. Bisset, then chairman of the BAAC, commenting on the
removal of Mary Queen of Scots' billiard table the night before her
execution. After her execution, her head was wrapped in the cloth
from that table*

Kick Backs
We do still get letters about 'kicks'. There's no explanation.
It's a little piece of dirt on the cue ball.
Dennis Taylor

Austentatious
Oh yes – it looks well mannered. It's like Jane Austen –
regulated hatred.
Clive Everton, during the 1981 Embassy World Championship

Punny
We weren't hoping for a boy or girl, we were just happy to
take pot luck.
Steve Davis, on the birth of his first child

Physical Attraction
Snooker is something to do with sex, beautiful legs and bottoms, as medieval women may have enjoyed [jousting] tournaments and some women enjoy boxing.
   A. S. Byatt

Happy Sad
I like playing in Sheffield . . . it's full of melancholy happy-go-lucky people.
   Alex Higgins

Spot On
Whoever called snooker 'chess with balls' was rude, but right.
   Clive James

Tradition
In the event of the yellow ball being involved in a foul stroke, it is the custom for the watchers to cry out the word 'bollocks'.
   From Savile Snooker

Anxiety Attack
It was very nerve-racking. I felt like a surgeon doing a brain operation. I broke out in a sweat when I had to cut it in half.
   Cue maker John Parris, on the strain of changing Steve Davis' cue from a one-piece to a two-piece

Nose Job

I managed to get my nose in front, and with a nose like mine, that's a big lead.

Mick Price, world no. 82, after defeating Dennis Taylor in the 1992 World Championship

Genesis Revisited

On the eighth day God created Alex Higgins.

Slogan on T-shirt

3. Invective

Sorry Is The Hardest Word

Alex [Higgins] is very good at apologising, but then he's had plenty of practice.

Dennis Taylor

Personality Clash

Frankly, I'd rather have a drink with Idi Amin.

Alex Higgins on Steve Davis. Davis' reply was: 'That's probably because Amin buys more rounds!'

Put Down

We're not into minority sports.

Barry Hearn, asked if he was going to bid for Manchester United

Divine Ambition

I hope he [Barry Hearn] doesn't go out of snooker, because the only other job he would want is God's, and that will take a bit of getting.

Cliff Wilson

Mixed Message

So eventually, as we go to shake hands, I'd kick him right in the nuts.

Cliff Thorburn, known as 'The Grinder' and 'The Methodical Mountie', on his strained relations with Alex Higgins

Big Mouth

Spectator: Do you think you can get it [the snooker ball] in?
Dennis Taylor: Well, I could if the pockets were as big as your mouth.

Side Issues
The only side he [Alex Higgins] hasn't attempted is suicide.
Ray Reardon

So Cruel
A lot of people are using two-piece cues nowadays. Alex Higgins hasn't got one, because they don't come with instructions.
Steve Davis

Strong Stomach
Someone threw a petrol bomb at him and he drank it.
Frank Carson, on Alex Higgins

Mental Health
Alex [Higgins] is remarkable, you know. If Alex went to a psychiatrist, the psychiatrist would have to see a psychiatrist.
Ronnie Harper

Hanging On
Alex Higgins should have been here today, but he was launching a ship in Belfast and they couldn't get him to let go of the bottle.
Dennis Taylor

Theatre Nights
Call yourself a pro, you couldn't pot a plant.
Taunt from heckler

4. TV Dinners

Reprise
If you didn't see Davis against Hendry last night, then you can see it again now.
BBC television announcer

Role Reversal
Well, valour was the better part of discretion there.
Jack Karnehm

Conflict Resolution
He'll have no trouble in solving the solution.
Jack Karnehm

Portrait Of An Artist As A Young Man
I think he's great. He's got fewer zits than me and he's much better looking.
Stephen Hendry, on his Spitting Image *puppet*

Inevitable
When a one-legged snooker player from Iceland is drawn against a man who won the World Championship three times, there can only be one result. Brynjar Valdimarsson beat John Spencer, 5-1.
David Hunn

Early Warning Signals
John Spencer can't really afford to be 5-1 down at such an early stage.
Jack Karnehm

Different Strokes
Billiards is very similar to snooker, except there are only three balls and no one watches it.
Steve Davis

Against The Odds
It was like Sergeant Bilko beating Ali over the full fifteen.
Frank Keating, on Dennis Taylor's win over Steve Davis in the 1985 Embassy World Championship Final

Virtue
I said No to Tony Knowles.
Slogan on T-shirt after Knowles remarked that he rated girls, not out of ten, but out of two – those who say yes, and those who say no

Peerless
Steve Davis is acknowledged by his peers to be the peerless master.
John McCririck

Either Or
Hurricane Higgins can either win or lose this final match tomorrow.
Archie McPherson

Every Face Tells A Story
You can tell when Kirk [Stevens] is thinking. When he is not thinking, he looks like an Easter Island statue with a sinus problem. When he is thinking, he still looks like that, but licks his lips.
   Clive James

Inevitably
This said, the inevitable failed to happen.
   John Pulman

Time Travel
Sometimes the deciding frame's always the toughest to win.
   Dennis Taylor

Shock News
And now, snooker. And Steve Davis has crashed out of the UK Billiards Championship.
   Allan Taylor

Divine Wisdom?
He won't feel the pressure as much as the more less-experienced players.
   David Icke (before he claimed to be the son of God)

13

Tennis Theatricals

In theory, the tennis courts are a theatre in which an attempt is made to establish superior skills. In practice, they are often the forum where an engaging battle of wits can occur, with the battle on the scoreboard being the last thing on anyone's mind. Sometimes the results are bemusing. More often, as we shall see, they are amusing.

1. Players

Problems
Louise Brough cannot serve at the moment; because she hasn't got any balls.
Rex Alston

Abusive
I'm telling you, this guy [John McEnroe] can't pick his nose without people booing him.
Peter Fleming

Zooroapa
If you put monkeys on to play, they'd still pack Centre Court at Wimbledon.
Neale Fraser

Limited Vocabulary
Good shot, bad luck and hell are the five basic words to be used in tennis.
Virginia Graham

Hair-raising
Hair [John McEnroe] like badly-turned broccoli.
Clive James

Silence Is Golden
When Ilie Nastase plays John McEnroe, it's the only time the
crowd call for silence.
Jerry Girard

Marital Problems
An otherwise happily married couple may turn a mixed
doubles game into a scene from *Who's Afraid of Virginia Woolf?*
Rod Laver

Sticky Situation
Kathy Jordan has a frying pan grip.
Rex Bellamy

Noah's Lark
[Yannick] Noah always beats Curren, he has a sort of
Houdini against him.
David Lloyd

Wind Problems
Billie Jean King has always been conscious of wind on the
centre court.
Dan Maskell

Blood Brothers
The Gullikson twins, Tim and Tom, are both from Wisconsin.
Dan Maskell

The Battle Of The Sexes
She's a great player, for a gal. But no woman can beat a male
player who knows what he's doing. I'll put Billie Jean and all
the other Women's Libbers back where they belong – in the
kitchen and the bedroom.
*Bobby Riggs, before his match with Billie Jean King. King won
in straight sets*

P. S.
There is no doubt that Billie Jean's victory was a big one for
the women's movement and for all women. One guy said to
me, after the match, 'That set my marriage back ten years –
and I've only been married two years.'
Bobby Riggs, after his defeat

Bacon and Egg

I use the analogy of bacon and egg to describe the difference between involvement and commitment in sport – the hen is involved in the process through laying the egg, but the pig is totally committed!

Martina Navratilova

Mixed Review

Never has sport produced such an enigmatic man [Ilie Nastase]. For while nature endowed him with the golden gift of instinctive athleticism, she left him a little short in stability.

Laurie Pignon

The Good Food Diet

There are a few. There's one with my name. I mean I just love the food, the Italian food.

Gabriela Sabatini, when asked her favourite restaurant in Rome

Slow Motion

Charlie Pasarell moves so slowly between points, that at times he seems to be flirting with reverse gear.

Rex Bellamy

Jargon

Anticipation at the net is just a woman's fancy word for guessing right.

Bill Tilden

Foot Fault

The only way to beat Martina now is to run over her foot in the car park.

Pam Shriver

Lloyd's of Wimbledon

Not since Betty Grable has so much been written about a pair of legs as John Lloyd's.

Taki

Master Tactician

There are few tactical rules for mixed doubles. One is to hit the girl whenever possible.

Bill Tilden

The French Connection

She's French. And I'm still learning the culture.

*Jeff Tarango, asked what he thought about his wife throwing a
punch at the umpire when he stormed off court 13 at Wimbledon
in 1995, following his clash with the umpire because of a
disputed call*

Freudian Slip

She [Martina Navratilova] won in straight sex…sets, 6-2, 6-0.

Joanne Watson

Betty Blue

Miss [Betty] Stove seems to have gone off the boil.

Peter West

2. Media Monitoring

Nasty and Nastier

When Nastase is winning, he's objectionable. When he's
losing, he's highly objectionable.

Adrian Clark

Spinning Wheel

Kriek, receiving service, spun his racket as if using a manual
food mixer.

Rex Bellamy

Apache
Bjorn Borg looks like a hunch-backed, jut-bottomed version of Elizabeth Scott impersonating a bearded Apache princess.
Clive James

All You Need Is Love
Tennis players start with love.
Colin M. Jarman

Mixed Metaphor?
Lendl remains as calm as the proverbial iceberg.
Dan Maskell

Line-up
Behind every tennis player there is another tennis player.
Bob McPhee

The Dracula Complex
He has been bitten...he has been beaten, I should say, by Ilie Nastase.
American newsreader

RRRRRRRR
He's wanked . . . ranked well outside the world's 250.
Gary Richardson from Sporting Gaffes

Not What It Seems
The British boys are adopting the attacking position – [Mark] Cox up.
Dan Maskell

The Battle Of The Bulge
Todd Nelson is coffee coloured – medium roast – and has such well-developed muscles that one wonders how his skin takes the strain.
Rex Bellamy

Insulation
Kathy Jordan's racket arm bears not only a wristlet, but also an elbow bandage; which means that her arm looks like a lagged cold water pipe.
Rex Bellamy

Oh, Really
We don't always get from slow motion the pace at which
they play.
John Barrett

Charisma Deficit
Like a Volvo, Bjorn Borg is rugged, has good after-sales
service, and is very dull.
Clive James

Lapse Of Memory
Max Robertson [BBC commentator]: Who are they going to play
in the Final, do we know yet?
Christine Truman: This *is* the Final!

Strange But True?
When Martina is tense, it helps her to relax.
Dan Maskell

14
Sporting Miscellany

All sports personalities meek and tall share their reactions to triumphs and disasters in this assembly line of sporting quotations. Its aim is to entertain, rather than to educate. As will be evident, a lot of the time the personalities speak more from the heart than from the brain. Allow yourself to be enriched by the good, great or dubious deeds and laugh at their mishaps, misdemeanours or miscalculations.

1. Bodybuilding

Action Man
A muscle-bound man is worse than a skin-bound horse.
Bob Fitzsimmons

Gold Heart
The muscle-man with heart [Arnold Schwarzennegger] – and
pectorals – of gold.
Jack Kroll

2. Bowling

The Sound Of Silence
Ten-pin bowling is the quietest sport in the world, because
you can hear a pin drop.
Anon

On Hold
There is plenty of time to win this game, and to thrash the
Spaniards too.
*Sir Francis Drake, when told during a game of bowls that the
Spanish Armada was in sight*

Bowled Over
If John McEnroe turned up, we'd throw him out. We like
polite people in bowls.
Elsie Walters

Either Or
Life isn't all beer and skittles; some of us haven't touched a
skittle in years.
Anon

3. Climbing

River Deep. Mountain High
Climb every mountain, ford every burn,
Suffer a thrombosis, end up in an urn.
Arthur Marshall

Irrational

The late George Mallory said he climbed the mountain
'because it's there'. That makes as much sense as saying 'I eat
farmyard manure because it's organic'.

Anon

4. Croquet

Bright Sparks

As the sport needs a high degree of skill and intelligence, it is
not, therefore, going to attract the lower income groups.

Croquet Association

PR

I took to wearing shorts at tournaments to improve the image
of the game – to show that it wasn't just a collection of old
women of both sexes playing.

Richard Rothwell

To Hell With The Olympic Ideal

My doctor forbids me to play, unless I win.

Alexander Woollcott

5. Curling

Amongst Women
A female curling team is a group of sporting ladies with large besoms.
   Colin M. Jarman

By George
He's a' the curle! – the game is ended,
And that is all that was intended.
   George McIndoe, 1805

6. Cycling

An Englishman In Paris
The Tour de France is a totally different ball game from English cycle racing.
   Sidney Bennett

Cold Comfort
Talking of saddles; the first impression on climbing aboard is that it is slightly less comfortable than sitting astride a meat cleaver.
   Doug Ibbotson

7. Darts

If Only
If his [Eric Bristow's] dad had taken him to Sunday School instead of down the pub, it would have been better for all of us.
   Tony Brown

Gone Astray
In the World Darts Championship in 1982, Jocky Wilson missed when attempting to shake hands with an opponent.
   Craig Brown

Misconception
I was watching sumo wrestling on the television for two hours before I realised it was darts.
   Hattie Hayridge

Two In One
There's only one word for that – Magic Darts!
Tony Green

Calorie-challenged
He [Jocky Wilson] is 16 stain
Of fat and pain.
Bill Hill

Oral Tribute
He naething wins, wha' never ventures,
World Champion, Jocky [Wilson] – withoot yer dentures.
Angus McIntyre

Advantage
A good darts player who can count can always beat a brilliant
player who can't.
Leighton Rees

Rocket Man
If Eric Bristow was at Cape Canaveral, he'd take off before
the rocket.
Sid Waddell

Aggression
Tony Brown attacks his opponents the same way Desperate
Dan attacks cow pie.
Sid Waddell

Self-image
I have been described as fat, boozy, and toothless. That's
pretty accurate, I guess.
Jocky Wilson

All In The Mind
I had a bash at positive thinking, yoga, transcendental
meditation, even hypnotism. They only screwed me up, so
now I'm back to my normal routine – a couple of lagers.
Leighton Rees

8. One Man And His Dog

A Dog's Life 1
No dog can go as fast as the money you bet on him.
  'Bud' Flanagan

Adjusting The Odds
My grandfather couldn't prescribe a pill to make a greyhound run faster, but he could produce one to make the other five go slower.
  Benny Green

A Dog's Life 2
I use sportswriters and when we get a broken-down dog, we give him a typewriter.
  Ralph Ryan on the special hares he uses in training

Verdict
And now, here are the results of the Sheepdog Trials. All the sheepdogs were found not guilty.
  Keith Waterhouse

Nosy
Interviewer: What is a short head?
Interviewee: The dog's nose should be in front of the eyes.

9. Gliding

Upstanding
Gliders can keep it up all day.
  Colin M. Jarman

10. Gymnastics

Leap Of Fame
Romania's best-known vaulter since Dracula.
  Journalist on Nadia Comaneci, who became an instant superstar by posting the first ever perfect 10s in Olympic gymnastics competition

11. Hockey

Disappointment
I went to a fight the other night, and an ice-hockey game broke out.
Rodney Dangerfield

Good Coaching
I'll fine any of my players who wins the Lady Byng Trophy for ice hockey gentlemanly conduct.
Punch Imlach

Balance Of Payments
Canada is a country whose main exports are ice hockey players and cold fronts. Our two main imports are baseball players and acid rain.
Pierre Trudeau, former Canadian PM

12. Hunting

Ignorance Is Bliss
I have hunted deer on occasions, but they were not aware of it.
Felix Gear

13. Polo

Mission Impossible
Playing polo is like trying to play golf during an earthquake.
Sylvester Stallone

Cheapskate
Sex is just a poor man's polo.
Clifford Odets

14. Shooting

Breach Of Etiquette
Grouse shooting begins on August 12th. A grouse shot before that date tends to be very annoyed.
Michael Shea

15. Skating

Temptation
The thinner the ice, the more anxious everybody is to see if it
will bear [the weight].
Josh Billings

Thou Shalt Not Skate
No boy may go ice-skating on any water not passed by
the headmaster.
Notice at Eton School

Stand By She
My daughter's a really sweet girl.
*Tonya Harding's mother, after she recovered from collapsing live
on television in America whilst talking about her daughter – and
more particularly, about the controversy over a private home video
taken at Harding's wedding in which she appeared semi-naked
before 30 million television viewers, her wedding dress trailing
around her waist*

16. Skiing

Obstacle Course
Skiing combines outdoor fun with knocking down trees with
your face.
Dave Barry

Suggestive
Skiers do it on the piste.
Colin M. Jarman

And The Second Shall Be First
It's a race for second place, I'm going to win.
Bill Johnson

Gossip
People say it's piste-bashing by day and duvet-bashing
all night.
New Society

Catholic Ethos
It's unbecoming for a Cardinal to ski badly.
Pope John Paul II

17. Ski-jumping

This section is exclusively devoted to the most famous (or should that be infamous?) British ski-jumper – Eddie 'The Eagle' Edwards, who came last in both Olympic ski-jumps in 1988.

The Eagle Has Landed
His glasses are pink and white and as thick as the bottom of a Coca-Cola bottle, and when he puts his goggles over them, they mist up.
Chris Brasher

Political Analogies
He has done for British winter sports what Screaming Lord Sutch has done for the British electoral system.
Colin M. Jarman

Dismal
Mr Edwards' performance was the equivalent of a first ball duck in a Test match, two own goals in a Wembley Cup Final, or a first round of 168 in the Open Championships.
Ian Wooldridge

Dismissive
We have thousands of Eddie Edwards in Norway, but we never let them jump.
Torbjorn Yggeseth

18. Skydiving

No Second Chance
If at first you don't succeed – so much for skydiving.
Henny Youngman

19. Squash

Sadism
Squash – that's not exercise, it's flagellation.
Sir Noel Coward

20. Weight Lifting

Easily Pleased
Weight-lifters do it with a jerk.
Colin M. Jarman

21. Windsurfing

Take My Breath Away
Windsurfers do it standing up.
Colin M. Jarman

22. Wrestling

Adult Entertainment
Professional wrestling is just rehearsed acrobatics. It's not the sort of thing you would let your children go to see.
George Hackenschmidt

The Good Love Guide
A lot of wrestlers think they're God's gift to women. I'm different. I *know* I am!
Brian Maxime

Captive Audience
Professional wrestling's most mystifying hold is on its audience.
Luke Neely

23. Odds and Ends

Safety Measure
Never play 'rub bottoms' with a porcupine.
Jane Philbin

Odds On
Anybody can win, unless there happens to be a second entry.
George Ade

And The Last Shall Be . . .
Last guys don't finish nice.
Stanley Keeley

A Load Of Bull
What I like best about bullfighting is the big money and the small bulls.
Matador

So Sad To Watch Good Love Go Bad
I resigned as coach because of illness and fatigue. The fans were sick and tired of me.
John Ralston

Demythologising
What they say about footballers being ignorant is rubbish. I spoke to a couple yesterday, and they were quite intelligent.
Raquel Welch

Ego-centred
Remember, it doesn't matter whether you win or lose; what matters is whether *I* win or lose.
Darrin Weinberg

Only One Winner
If me and King Kong went into an alley, only one of us would come out. And it wouldn't be the monkey!
Lyle Alzado

High IQ
Al Davis is a very smart man. He's probably the only one who knows the serial number of the Unknown Soldier.
Sam Rutigliano

Energy Saver
The only exercise I ever get is taking the cuff-links out of one shirt and putting them in another.
Ring Lardner

Thwarted Ambitions
I wanted to be an Olympic swimmer, but I had some
problems with buoyancy.
Woody Allen

Don't Know What You Mean, Harry
Ah! Isn't that nice, the wife of the Cambridge President is
kissing the cox of the Oxford crew.
Harry Carpenter

Shooting From Above The Hip
I listened to a football coach who spoke straight from the
shoulder – at least, I could detect no higher origin in anything
he said.
Dixon Ryan Fox

Doggone
Vince Lombardi was fair, he treated us all the same –
like dogs.
Henry Jordan

Warning
Never play leapfrog with a unicorn.
Michael Shea

PART TWO

GREAT SPORTING SUPERMOUTHS OF OUR TIME

15

Walker the Talker

BBC motor racing commentator Murray Walker, otherwise known as 'Muddly Talker', is a television commentator who has left an enduring imprint on the sporting landscape with a series of memorable comments. Hence the slogan on T-shirts produced by the Murray Walker Fan Club: 'Unless I'm very much mistaken…I am very much mistaken.' Read on for some more Vintage Walkerisms.

1. The lead car is absolutely unique, except for the one behind it, which is identical.

2. Patrick Tambay's hopes, which were nil before, are absolutely zero now.

3. We're now on the 73rd lap and the next one will be the 74th.

4. If they have any shillelaghs in Suzuka, they'll be playing them tonight. (After Ireland's Eddie Irvine's sixth place in his first Grand Prix.)

5. He's watching us from hospital with his injured knee.

6. Mansell is slowing down, taking it easy. Oh no he isn't! It's a lap record.

7. Nigel Mansell – the Man of the Race – the Man of the Day – the Man from the Isle of Man.

8. You can't see a digital clock, because there isn't one.

9. He's obviously gone in for a wheel change. I say 'obviously', because I can't see it.

10. An Achilles heel for the McLaren team this year, and it's literally the heel, because it's the gear box.

11. It's not quite a curve, it's straight, actually.

12. And now the boot is on the other Schumacher.

13. I don't make mistakes. I make prophecies which immediately turn out to be wrong.

14. I make no apologies for their absence; I'm sorry they're not here.

15. The atmosphere is so tense, you could cut it with a cricket stump.

16. James has just nipped out to have a look at the far side of the circuit. (Describing how James Hunt would leave the commentary box to smoke a joint.)

Walker himself has been the subject of a memorable sports quote. Clive James said of him: 'In his quieter moments, he sounds as if his trousers are on fire.'

16

The Lowe-Down

While David Coleman is in a league of his own, another sports commentator, Ted Lowe ('Whispering Ted') runs the risk of being promoted (or is it relegated?) to this elite group. He has graced (disgraced?) the game of snooker with some vintage bloomers, of which the following are some of the classic 'Loweisms'.

1. Fred Davis, the doyen of snooker, now sixty-seven years of age and too old to get his leg over, prefers to use his left hand.

2. Oh, and that's a brilliant shot. The odd thing is, his mum's not very keen on snooker.

3. He's lucky in one sense and unlucky in the other.

4. Ninety-nine times out of a thousand, he would have potted that ball.

5. They're not only snooker players, they're engineers, taking apart a snooker cue and screwing it back again.

6. There is, I believe, a time limit for playing a shot. But I think it's true to say that nobody knows what that limit is.

7. And it is my guess that Steve Davis will try to score as many points as he can in this frame.

8. Steve Davis has a tough consignment in front of him.

9. That puts the game beyond reproach.

10. And Alex Higgins has literally come back from the dead.

11. All square all the way round.

12. Higgins first entered the Championship ten years ago; that was for the first time, of course.

13. It's not easy to get a snooker when there's only one ball on the table.

14. Jimmy White has that wonderful gift of being able to point his cue where he is looking.

15. One mistake here could win or lose the match either way.

16. And for those of you watching this in black and white, the pink sits behind the yellow.

17. Cliff Thorburn has been unsettled by the erratic but consistent potting of Perrie Mans.

18. Perrie Mans played a prominent part in this tournament in 1979. In fact, he won it.

19. This young man Jimmy White celebrated his twenty-second birthday literally four days ago.

20. The audience are literally electrified and glued to their seats.

21. Can Bill Werbeniuk be the second Canadian to rewrite the history books?

22. There he [Bill Werbeniuk] is, 20 stone of Canadian fat.

23. John Smyth [referee] is getting his little implement out.

24. That's inches away from being millimetre-perfect.

25. And Griffiths has looked at the blue four times now, and it still hasn't moved.

26. And that's the third time he's done that this session. He's missed his waistcoat pocket with the chalk.

27. The laughing Irish are smiling no longer.

28. Jimmy can make these balls talk, and what a story they're telling.

29. Alex, unlike many other professionals, adds a bit on his cue, rather than puts on an extension.

30. The audience is standing to relieve themselves.

31. Commentating isn't as simple as it sounds.

32. And Jimmy's potting is literally doing the commentary here.

33. Steve, with his sip of water, part of his make-up.

34. Well, the shot would have been safe if the red hadn't ended up over the pocket.

35. He's completely disappeared. He's gone back to his dressing-room. Nobody knows where he has gone.

36. It all adds up to a bit of fun. If commentators can't join in with the rest of the world, they must cry alone.

37. He's 40 points behind and there's only 51 points left on the table.

38. Of course, one of Stephen Hendry's greatest assets is his ability to score when he's playing.

39. Sometimes silence is golden. (Never did he speak a truer word. Pity he didn't follow his own advice more often!)

40. The butterflies are certainly flying around Higgins tonight.

The definitive Ted Lowe quote, though, must be: 'A little pale in the face, but then his [Jimmy White] name is White.'

17

On the Great Vine

The public face of BBC's snooker coverage is David Vine. While he is not in the same class in this respect as Ted Lowe, he has furnished some classic comments, some of which are listed over the page.

1. This match has gradually and suddenly come to a climax.

2. As for you, I don't know about me, I'm ready for bed.

3. Ray Reardon, one of the great Crucible champions, won it five times – when the Championship was played away from the Crucible.

4. 10-4 . . . and it could mean exactly what that means.

5. After twelve frames, they stand all square. The next frame, believe it or not, is the thirteenth.

6. Here we are in the Holy Land of Israel, a Mecca for tourists.

7. I'm speaking from a deserted and virtually empty Crucible Theatre.

8. No one came closer to winning the World title last year than the runner-up Dennis Taylor.

9. Suddenly Alex Higgins was 7-0 down.

10. But there was still the big prize money hanging there like a carrot waiting to be picked.

18
The Golden Foot in Mouth Award

Great sporting moments invariably produce great characters. One sports personality inextricably linked with sporting drama is David Coleman – a broadcaster whose name is synonymous with sporting howlers. The BBC commentator is remembered for a series of gaffes, with those over the page being my top 40 favourites.

1. This man could be a dark horse.

2. The late start is due to the time.

3. He's 31 this year; last year he was 30.

4. The pace of this match is really accelerating, by which I mean it is getting faster all the time.

5. Some names to look forward to – perhaps in the future.

6. Her time was 4 minutes 13 seconds, which she is capable of.

7. This could be a repeat of what will happen at the European Games, next week.

8. This race is all about racing.

9. David Bedford is the athlete of all time in the 1970s.

10. It doesn't mean anything, but what it does mean is that Abde Bile is very relaxed.

11. There is Brendan Foster, by himself, with 20,000 people.

12. And with an alphabetical irony, Nigeria follows New Zealand.

13. She's not Ben Johnson, but then, who is?

14. He just can't believe what's not happening to him.

15. For those of you watching who haven't TV sets, live commentary is on Radio Two.

16. Lasse Viren, the champion, came in fifth and ran a champion's race.

17. His brother failed, so let's see if he can succeed and maintain the family tradition.

18. They came through absolutely together, with Allan Wells in first place.

19. The reason she's so fast over hurdles is because she's so fast between them.

20. Panetta was the silver medallist in the European Championships, when he led all the way.

21. Manchester United are buzzing around the goalmouth like a lot of red bottles.

22. The news from the javelin is that it was won by the winning throw that we saw earlier.

23. Alan Pascoe could have won the gold, but he simply ran out of time.

24. Charlie Spedding believes in an even pace and hopes to run the second part of the race faster than the first.

25. It's a battle with himself and with the ticking finger of the clock.

26. There'll only be one winner in every sense of the word.

27. And the line-up for the Final of the women's 400 metres hurdles includes three Russians, two East Europeans, a Pole, a Swede and a Frenchman.

28. There's going to be a real ding-dong when the bell goes.

29. You've got to hand it to Gonzalez, once he saw it was possible, he saw his chance and made it possible.

30. He's even smaller in real life than he is on the track.

31. Dusty Hare kicked 19 of the 17 points.

32. Both of the Villa scorers – Withe and Mortimer – were born in Liverpool, as was the Villa manager – Ron Saunders – who was born in Birkenhead.

33. Coe has made absolutely no move at all down the back straight.

34. The big guns haven't pulled all the stops out.

35. He won the bronze medal in the 1976 Olympics, so he is used to being out in the front.

36. Lilian Board's great strength is her great strength.

37. The ball has broken 50-50 for Keegan.

38. Bradford, who had gone up from 200 metres to 400, found it hard going and for the last 100 metres was always going backwards.

39. Kevin Reeves, who's just turned 22, providing that an ill wind blows nobody any good.

40. One of the great unknown champions, because very little is known about him.

First Among Equals
It's very difficult to single out the one classic Coleman howler, so I've opted for a dead heat:
'That's the magic of television – I've just heard over the headphones that Noalto was third.'
'Don't tell those coming the final result of the fantastic match, but let's just have another look at Italy's winning goal.'